AF470632
Berlitz
SARDINIA
POCKET GUIDE

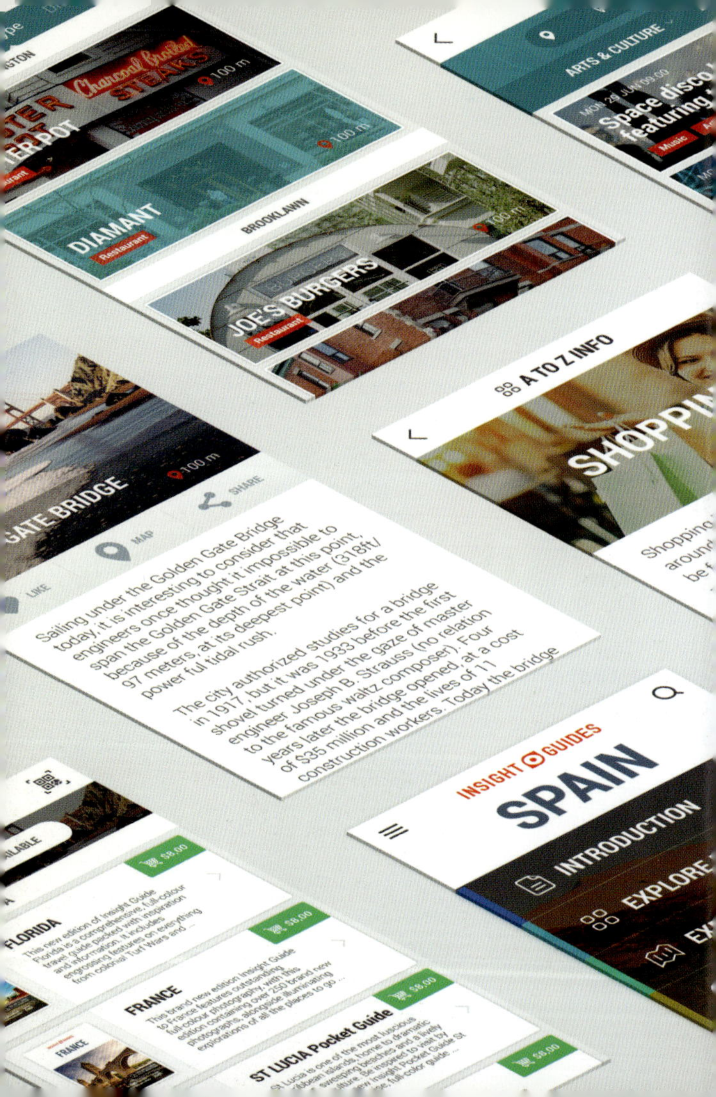
Charcoal Broiled STEAKS
100 m
DIAMANT
Restaurant
BROOKLAWN
100 m
JOE'S BURGERS
Restaurant
ARTS & CULTURE
Space disco
featuring
Music
A TO Z INFO
SHOPPIN
Shopping
around
be f
GATE BRIDGE
100 m
SHARE
MAP
LIKE
Sailing under the Golden Gate Bridge today, it is interesting to consider that engineers once thought it impossible to span the Golden Gate Strait at this point, because of the depth of the water (318ft/ 97 meters, at its deepest point) and the power ful tidal rush.
The city authorized studies for a bridge in 1917, but it was 1933 before the first shovel turned under the gaze of master engineer Joseph B. Strauss (no relation to the famous waltz composer). Four years later the bridge opened, at a cost of $35 million and the lives of 11 construction workers. Today the bridge
INSIGHT GUIDES
SPAIN
INTRODUCTION
EXPLORE
FLORIDA
This new edition of Insight Guide Florida is a comprehensive, full-colour travel guide packed with inspiration and information. It includes engrossing features on everything from colonial Turf Wars and ...
$8.00
FRANCE
This brand new edition Insight Guide to France features outstanding full-colour photography, with this edition containing over 250 brand new photographs, alongside illuminating explorations of all the places to go ...
$8.00
ST LUCIA Pocket Guide
St Lucia is one of the most luscious Caribbean islands, home to dramatic sweeping beaches and a lively culture. Be inspired to visit by this new Insight Pocket Guide St ...
$8.00

Walking Eye
mobile app

Discover the world's best destinations with the Insight Guides Walking Eye app, available to download for free in the App Store and Google Play.

The container app provides easy access to fantastic free content on events and activities taking place in your current location or chosen destination, with the possibility of booking, as well as the regularly-updated Insight Guides travel blog: Inspire Me. In addition, you can purchase curated, premium destination guides through the app, which feature local highlights, hotel, bar, restaurant and shopping listings, an A to Z of practical information and more. Or purchase and download Insight Guides eBooks straight to your device.

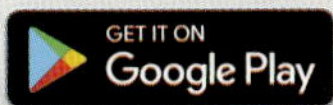

TOP 10 ATTRACTIONS

CAGLIARI
Admire the Sardinian capital's medieval Castello district. See page 27.

NURAGHE SANTU ANTINE
Visit this mysterious megalithic site. See page 79.

SUPRAMONTE
Boasts spectacular hiking for all levels. See page 55.

THARROS, SINIS PENINSULA
The seaside remains of the Punic-Roman city of Tharros. See page 48.

MADDALENA ARCHIPELAGO
Join a cruise at Palau to experience the beauty of this island chain. See page 65.

GROTTA DI NETTUNO
The island's most spectacular cave. See page 73.

GOLFO DI OROSEI
This lovely stretch of coast is best seen from the water. See page 59.

CARLOFORTE
The pretty port makes a good base for exploring the island of San Pietro. See page 39.

BOSA
Narrow streets lead through the picturesque old town. See page 74.

ALGHERO
Enjoy Alghero's relaxed pace, with its fortified walls and Historic Centre. See page 69.

A PERFECT DAY

9.00am

Breakfast

In Alghero, take breakfast at Caffè Latino on the ramparts at Bastioni Magellano, enjoying views over the port.

2.00pm

Castelsardo

Explore the steep lanes and enjoy sea views from the fortress town of Castelsardo. Shop for *artigianato* or handicrafts (basketwork, coral and ceramics) in the lower town, before climbing up to the castle and its Basketweaving Museum. Watch women basket-weaving on their doorsteps and bargain for their wares.

10.00am

To Sassari

Head northeast from Alghero on SS127 and follow signs for Sassari. Spend time sightseeing, shopping or soaking up Sardinian town life from the palm-shaded gardens of the Piazza d'Italia.

12 noon

Lunch

Lunch in atmospheric L'Assassino trattoria in Sassari or you may prefer to take the SS200 north passing Sorso, whose surrounding vineyards produce fine Cannonau wine, and try Ristorante Il Cormorano in Castelsardo.

IN SARDINIA

Northwest coast

Return to the SS200 and follow the coastal road in the Porto Torres direction. Secluded beaches give way to the busy seaside resorts of Platamona and Marina di Sorso. Give industrial Porto Torres a wide berth (keen sightseers should return another day for the Basilica and Roman remains) and head south to Alghero on the SP42.

Nightlife

Try the lively bars on the seafront or the open-air ones in the centre.

Fairy houses

On the road to Alghero, about 10km (6 miles) before you reach the city, stop briefly to explore the Anghelu Ruju Necropolis, with around 40 rock-cut tombs known as *domus de janas* (fairy houses), dating from the late Neolithic era.

Sunset aperitivo

Back in Alghero, enjoy fresh-fruit cocktails and fabulous views of the sunset on sea-facing Bastioni Marco Polo.

Dinner

Prolong the views and dine on suckling pig, Catalan lobster or simple pasta at one of the restaurants along Bastioni Marco Polo.

CONTENTS

INTRODUCTION

In 1921, when D.H. Lawrence decided he needed a break from his home in Sicily, he opted for an island 'outside the circuit of civilisation'. After an abundance of culture in Sicily and other parts of Italy, he was seeking a place of simplicity, or, as he described Sardinia, 'belonging to nowhere'.

Some 90 years on, Sardinia still feels quite distinct from the rest of Italy. In common with other Mediterranean islands it has been occupied, colonised and exploited by successive waves of invaders. Few of these powers saw it as anything more than a useful trading post at the crossroads of crucial Mediterranean sea routes. The Phoenicians plundered it for the rich ore deposits in the west, the Romans exploited it for grain, otherwise regarding it as an unhealthy backwater, the Spaniards treated it as a remote European outpost; Nelson coveted the island as a naval base, but failed to persuade the British to buy it. While other Mediterranean islands have adopted the character of their colonisers – Malta becoming British, Crete Greek, the Balearics Spanish, just to name a few – Sardinia has retained a remarkable cultural identity. It may not have the sophistication or the wealth of sights that greet you in Sicily or cities on the mainland, but it is a land that is truly steeped in tradition and custom. Local dialects

Beach bliss

In the high season (late June to early September) space on the easily accessible beaches is at a premium, but travellers who are prepared to negotiate unsigned dirt tracks or scramble down steep paths are likely to find space in secluded coves.

still thrive, artisan skills have been revived, and religious and pagan traditions are celebrated by more than 1,000 annual festivals. Moreover, each region retains its culinary specialities, from elaborate home-made bread and pastries to suckling pig slowly roasted and served on a bed of myrtle leaves.

TOURISM TODAY

Much, of course, has changed since Lawrence's day. Since the 1960s the international jet set have been flocking to the Costa Smeralda, mere mortals to less famous resorts on low-cost airlines. Brochure descriptions of Sardinia as 'a slice of the Seychelles' or 'Italy's Caribbean' are not complete hyperbole. It would be hard to find a concentration of such enticing beaches anywhere else in the Mediterranean. The sands are white, the waters come in every conceivable shade of blue and green and the wind-sculpted rocks, cliffs, dunes and marshes

Multihued Bosa

provide stunning and continually shifting vistas. The island has 1,800km (1,125 miles) of shoreline, which is a quarter of the entire Italian seaboard. The chiselled nature of the coast, with its rocky inlets, bays and promontories, accounts for this surprisingly high figure. Sheer cliffs and lack of access have largely precluded heavy development and though recent years have seen self-catering complexes sprouting on hills behind, large tracts of the shore are still almost untouched. Some beaches, like Chia in the south and Piscinas in the southwest, stretch for miles. Moreover, Sardinia has 300 sunny days a year and reliably hot, dry and sunny weather from May to September. From a summer-only, stay-put beach holiday destination, Sardinia is now attracting tourists all year round. Late spring and early autumn are ideal times for hikers, bikers and others who want to explore the island without the crowds. Beach resorts close down for the winter, but town accommodation is always available, and Alghero, well served by Ryanair, is lively all year round.

The island is a haven for water sports enthusiasts. The offshore breezes, particularly in the north, provide perfect conditions for sailing and windsurfing and the translucent waters that wash the shores have given rise to numerous diving centres all around the island. Many resorts are launching pads for boat trips to explore coves, inlets, islands and otherwise inaccessible beaches.

Since most visitors escape to Sardinia for beaches or sporting activities, the cultural attractions are rarely crowded. The most abundant and distinctive of the island's monuments are the *nuraghi*, or stone towers, dating from the Bronze Age. These mysterious megaliths, built as dwellings, fortifications and sanctuaries, offer a tantalising glimpse of this early civilisation. The architectural legacy from later Mediterranean occupiers lies scattered around the island: Carthaginian and Roman remains, Pisan-Romanesque churches and Spanish-style dwellings and monuments.

Sardinia is the second largest island in the Mediterranean (after Sicily) and many tourists, daunted by its size, stay put in one resort. Main roads, however, are surprisingly fast and it would be a pity to miss out on a foray into the mountainous interior, a visit to one of the historic town centres or a day's merrymaking at one of the many festivals. Among the most flamboyant of Sardinia's celebrations are the Sa Sartiglia, a medieval procession and tournament at Oristano and the S'Ardia at Sédilo, featuring frenetic horse racing, not unlike that of Siena's Palio.

FLORA, FAUNA AND THE INTERIOR

The population of the island is over 1.6 million, with sheep outnumbering Sards by three to one. Inland, the impression is one of emptiness and space. What was once thick woodland is now pungent *macchia*, a mixed vegetation of myrtle, juniper, arbutus, broom and cistus, that presents a riot of colour in spring. The varied landscape provides habitats for some rare species including mouflon, the wild long-horned sheep, the small Sardinian deer (*cervo sardo*) and the *cavallini*, the miniature

Shopping in a Nuoro market

wild horses that roam on the Giara di Gésturi plain. More conspicuous and exotic are the large flocks of pink flamingoes seen on the lagoons of Oristano and Cagliari.

The landscape is rarely dramatic but the wild Gennargentu mountains in the heart of the island provide scenic hiking, trekking and rockclimbing. Isolated villages, previously the home of shepherds and bandits, are slowly opening to tourism, offering guided treks, archaeological tours and other rural diversions. While formerly most of the tourist accommodation was located on the coast, there is now a large choice of *agriturismi* (farm properties) or Bed and Breakfasts for those who want a taste of rural life. It is inland that you will find the typical Sard. Over the centuries invaders who settled on the shores forced the coastal dwellers to migrate inland and raise livestock for a living. Shaped by centuries of foreign domination, the inhabitants of the rural villages, particularly in Nuoro province, are fiercely proud, with a passion for freedom and independence. Indeed, most islanders regard themselves as Sardinians first, and Italians very much second. In the mountain villages where life has changed little for centuries, or is only just beginning to do so, local people are noticeably more insular and less ebullient than the typical Italian. But like all Sards, they are generous and welcoming to visitors.

A BRIEF HISTORY

Sardinia's strategic maritime setting between Africa, Spain and Italy has always played a crucial role in the island's history. Over the centuries the island suffered the rampages of a succession of foreign invaders: Phoenicians, Carthaginians, Romans, Vandals, Pisans, Genoese and Spaniards. Each new arrival made its mark on the island, but the richest legacy was left by settlers from the dawn of history.

EARLY SETTLERS

Mystery surrounds the origins of the first settlers on the island, but evidence suggests tribes from the Italian mainland or North Africa were inhabiting caves around 6000BC. By the 4th millennium BC, settlers were creating villages of circular wood huts on stone foundations. Elaborate rock-cut tombs, known as *domus de janas* (fairy houses), date from this era, and from these evolved the *tombe di gigante* (giants' tombs), burial chambers fronted by a huge carved stele. Construction techniques for dwellings gradually developed and culminated in the evocative *nuraghi*. Dating from

Nuraghe Santu Antine

1800BC–900BC, these conical roofed towers were built with large blocks of stone without the use of mortar. Some 7,000 survive on the island, varying greatly in function and complexity. The majority are simple and compact, others such as Santu Antine at Torralba and Su Nuraxi at Barumini stand three storeys high and appear to have been fortresses, with watchtowers, bastions and other defences. Bronze statuettes unearthed at Nuragic villages offer a glimpse of a layered and complex society of aristocrats, warriors, shepherds and farmers. Sadly there is no written record from this mysterious era, but given that some of the names of the *nuraghi* have no Greek, Punic or Latin origin, the well-known expression *'il vero Sardo'* (the true Sardinian) may connote a true ethnic survival.

The first recorded settlers on the island, around 800BC, were the Phoenicians, who traded extensively in metals and established coastal settlements in the south and west. Threatened by local rebellions they appealed to the Carthaginians who gradually appropriated the coasts. The most conspicuous legacy of Punic rule are the ruins of the ancient cities of Nora, Tharros and Sulcis (present-day Sant' Antióco).

Roman baths at Fordongianus

ROME AND THE AFTERMATH

Victory over Carthage in the Punic Wars led to Rome's brutal 700-year rule of Sardinia. In 227BC the island became Rome's second province, along with Corsica. In the first century or so, rebellions were quelled, and after a particularly sharp revolt in 176BC many of the islanders were deported as slaves by the Romans. By 46BC, Cagliari had become an important port of the Roman fleet. The islanders adopted the Latin language, but the Roman remains on the island (and notably the amphitheatre at Cagliari, the ancient city of Nora and the Roman colony at Porto Torres) speak more of the might of the Empire and the wealth of its own expatriates than to any lasting beneficial influence on the islanders.

With the final collapse of the Roman Empire in the west, Sardinia, along with other Mediterranean islands and the whole of Roman North Africa, became a victim of barbarian raids. Vandal rule lasted until AD534, by which time Western Europe was fragmented into motley barbarian states. The most civilised European power was the surviving Roman Empire in the east, or the Byzantine Empire, which then theoretically held sway over Sardinia and other distant western outposts. But in the early 700s, during the massive surge of Islam following the death of Mohammed, great armies of Saracens (Arab Muslims) streamed across North Africa and into the Iberian Peninsula. There was little or no Christian resistance; in 711 Cagliari was sacked and occupied, and for the next two centuries the island suffered repeated Arab invasions.

Island backwater

The island of Sardinia was regarded by the Roman administration as an unhealthy backwater, exemplified by an act of the Emperor Tiberius who conscripted 4,000 Jewish freedmen to service there.

CHRISTIAN INFLUENCE

Despite the ongoing Arab incursions, it was in the 9th century that records first made mention of a *giudice* or governing judge of the land. By the early 11th century the island was divided into four *giudicati* or states: Cagliari, Arborea, Gallura and Torres, each controlled by its own *giudice*. The system was the greatest legacy of Byzantium, which was renowned for its legal and bureaucratic administration. But

⊙ ELEONORA D'ARBOREA

The warrior Queen of Arborea was one of the most significant lawmakers of medieval Europe. She is best known for the famous *Carta de Logu*, which was adopted as the basis for the whole island's legal code. Initiated by her father, the *giudice* Mariano IV, but promulgated during Eleonora's reign in 1392, the code consisted of 198 chapters and regulated matters as varied as crime, civil wrongs and the legal position of women, children and slaves. In 1421 this remarkably progressive code was adopted by the Aragonese rulers and remained the bedrock of the island's law until the 19th century. Eleonora was also renowned for her remarkable skill and energy in defending the independence of Arborea from Aragonese control. Married to a Genoese aristocrat of the Doria family, she spent much of her early life in Genoa but returned to Sardinia after the assassination of her brother to become Giudichessa of Arborea, and ruled Arborea from 1383 until 1404 when she died of the plague. After her death the resistance gradually yielded and Sardinia fell to the Aragonese. A 19th-century statue of Eleonora, holding a scroll with the *Carta de Logu*, can be seen in the Piazza Eleonora in Oristano.

Fresco in Bosa's church of
Nostra Signora di Regnos Altos

by this time the papacy, along with the Holy Roman Empire, had itself become a political power. Genoa and Pisa, the two rival dominant Italian maritime powers in the western basin of the Mediterranean, were given papal permission to recover lands from the infidel. Hence, Pisa captured Sardinia from the Muslims in 1016, as part of a Christian regeneration in southern Europe. Pisan occupation of the island is graphically illustrated by military architecture, and notably the medieval fortifications in the old quarter of Cagliari. The next 200 years or so were characterised by shifts of control and influence between Pisa, Genoa and, in the latter part, Aragon, aided and abetted by the Vatican, the Holy Roman Empire and the Sardinians themselves. This instability between the big powers was by and large ended in 1326 when Alfonso IV of Aragon, again with papal backing, effectively took possession of the island after a two-year siege of Cagliari.

16th-century map of
Sardinia and Corsica

The late 14th century saw the rise of Eleonora d'Arborea, Sardinia's heroine who is often likened to Boudicca or Joan of Arc. Her death marked the climax of a glorious but brief period of Sardinian resistance.

SPANISH RULE

Following the marriage of Ferdinand of Aragon and Isabella of Castile in 1479 and hence the unification of the whole of Spain, Sardinia became a province ruled by a Spanish viceroy. The notable events on the island during this period are little more than symptomatic of the European superpowers' struggle for supremacy in the Mediterranean. In 1541 Charles V, king of Spain and Holy Roman Emperor, visited the island with a vast fleet, en route to flush out a notorious corsair, Hassan Aga, who had pillaged Christian ships for his Muslim master. In 1553 Olbia was destroyed by the Turks, who had allied with France against Spain, and half its population was enslaved or deported. Under the feudal system on the island, land was distributed to Spanish nobles who enjoyed absolute power but left the everyday running of their dominions to officials of their own choice. Unsurprisingly, Sardinia became in essence a sleepy, uncared-for backwater of the enormous Spanish Empire. Its rulers cared more for its American colonies (the source of its opulence) and its intractable politico-religious problems than their remote European possessions.

The War of Spanish Succession, fought between Spain and her rival European powers, largely determined the state of Europe until the Napoleonic Wars. Sardinia, however, was an exception. At the close of the war, through the Treaties of Utrecht and Rastadt (1713 and 1714), the island became part of the Austrian Empire – the Holy Roman part of the erstwhile Spanish Empire – while Sicily passed to the House of Savoy. In 1717 Spain took back Sardinia from the Empire but three years later renounced her claim to the island, which then passed to the House of Savoy. In exchange, Sicily was then ceded to the Austrian Empire by the Savoys.

THE KINGDOM OF SARDINIA

The new Kingdom of Sardinia, ruled over in 1720 by Vittorio Amedeo II, comprised the island along with Savoy's enlarged Italian possessions in Savoy, Piedmont and Montferrat. A power of growing significance in Europe, Savoy added further territorial gains during the 18th century. Yet despite policies of investment and limited reform, Sardinia remained feudal and much of its population was opposed to any kind of foreign administration. Centuries of robbery and violence had arisen in the main from hunger and vendetta, the latter being rooted in fierce loyalty to friend and family. It was against this historical background and the slow pace of reform that Sardinia in the 18th century saw an escalation of banditry; clan warfare, kidnapping and robbery were rife.

During the Napoleonic Wars, Sardinia, uniquely in mainland and Mediterranean Europe, remained unconquered by Bonaparte. In 1793 the French were repulsed

Nelson's wish

Nelson coveted the island for the British, writing in despatches: 'If we could possess one island, Sardinia, we should want neither Malta, nor any other'.

from Cagliari by the islanders, and in 1798 Sardinia, along with the kingdom of Sicily, formally entered the war against the French. Nelson's flagship berthed at Sant'Antioco on its way to the Battle of the Nile and his fleet was often present around the Straits of Bonifacio in the run-up to the Battle of Trafalgar. The relative security of the island enabled the Savoy royal family to take refuge there during the Napoleonic Wars. In 1815, as part of the post-Napoleonic settlement, Genoa was added to the kingdom that became known as 'Piedmont Sardinia'.

The Savoy rulers were in the main hostile to the escalating liberal movements in Europe and moved only slowly to improve the political and economic conditions of the kingdom. Progress, however, was made under King Carlo Felice (1821–31), who improved the infrastructure and built the Carlo Felice highway running the length of the island (the present-day SS131). Under his successor, Carlo Alberto (1831–49), the feudal system was finally abolished.

UNIFICATION

From 1851 to 1861 Sardinia was in the forefront of the Risorgimento (the movement for Italian unification). Carlo Alberto enhanced the cause under Piedmont hegemony by granting a constitution in 1848 and resisting Austrian power in Italy in the first War of Independence (1848–9). His son, Vittorio Emanuele, supported Piedmont's prime minister, Count Cavour, in his diplomatic manoeuvres to unite the northern Italian states in the push for unification. But southern Italy, known since 1815 as the Kingdom of the Two Sicilies and with its capital in Naples, had to be wrested by conquest from its Bourbon masters. Giuseppe Garibaldi led the famous expedition of *I Mille* (The Thousand). Starting in 1860, it took him just five months to conquer Sicily and the kingdom of Naples, only halting his march on the papal states to enable Cavour's northern armies to finish the job. On 25 October 1860

Garibaldi handed southern Italy to Cavour. In 1861 Vittorio Emanuele II became king of a united Italy and the Kingdom of Sardinia came to an end.

Sardinia was the last home of Garibaldi, the most distinguished soldier of the movement and one of the most skilful guerilla generals in history.

FROM UNIFICATION TO THE PRESENT

19th-century railway remains at Spiaggia Piscinas

Since Unification, Sardinia has had to adapt to the challenge of being part of a major nation state while advancing its own particular interests and retaining its own cultural identity. In the early stages, entrenched colonial attitudes prevailed and much of its resources, such as its forests, were plundered. Mussolini advanced radical social and economic initiatives. Rivers were systematically channelled and dammed, land drainage schemes were carried out and three new towns, Carbonia, Fertilia and Arborea, were created. Following World War II the American Rockefeller Foundation piloted a successful scheme to exterminate malaria, which had plagued the island for centuries. Coastal marshes were gradually reclaimed, and could be developed for agriculture and holiday resorts.

World War II saw Cagliari suffer heavy bombing, which flattened over half the city. In the wake of the war, movements to advance the independence of the island bore fruit when Sardinia was finally granted a substantial degree of autonomy.

Messages in murals, Orgosolo

Under a special statute of 1948, Sardinia was to be 'an autonomous region with its own legal status'; it now has its own government, the Giunta, appointed by a regional council, elected by proportional representation.

In the 1960s tourism took off with the development of the Costa Smeralda. The glittering coastline continues to entice celebrities, but in 2006 the Sardinian president, Renato Soru, rocked the boat by imposing swingeing taxes on second homes on the coast, large non-Sardinian yachts and private aircraft. Soru also angered local developers by prohibiting construction of new property in undeveloped areas within 2km (1.25miles) of the coastline. The centre-left governor was ousted in the 2009 local elections by Ugo Cappellacci, a member of Silvio Berlusconi's 'People of Freedom' party, who happened to be the son of the former premier's fiscal adviser. One of Cappellacci's first moves was to scrap Soru's taxes on yachts and private jets. Continued political instability gave birth to the Canton Marittimo movement which, in the run-up to the regional elections in 2014, provocatively suggested that Sardinia should be sold to Switzerland and become its 27th canton. Amid widespread disillusionment, Francesco Pigliaru of the Democratic Party became the new president of the region, followed in 2019 by the Sardinian Action Party's Christian Solinas.

HISTORICAL LANDMARKS

6000–1800BC Neolithic era; tribes settle on the island; first villages built.

4000–3000 BC Ozieri culture.

1800–900 BC Nuragic era; large tower-like structures *(nuraghi)* built.

800 BC Phoenicians set up trading posts on the island.

7th century BC Greek colonies founded.

6th century BC Carthaginians appropriate coastal regions.

AD227 Sardinia becomes a Roman province.

AD456 Sardinia annexed by the Vandals.

Early 700s Arabs pillage the island, and seize control of part of it in 752.

9th century Documents record a *'giudice'*, a governing figure.

1016 Pisa captures Sardinia from the Muslims.

1323–6 The Aragonese take control of Sardinia, with papal backing.

1383–1404 Reign of Eleonora; she promulgates *Carta di Logu* (1392).

1479 Sardinia becomes a province of newly united Spain.

1713–1720 Sardinia ceded to Austria, then to Savoy.

1792–1805 Sardinia remains unconquered during the Napoleonic Wars.

1815 Sardinia becomes part of an enlarged Kingdom of Piedmont Sardinia.

1861 Sardinia becomes part of the newly unified Italy.

1943 Cagliari suffers major bomb destruction in World War II.

1948 Sardinia is made an autonomous region.

1960s Development of Costa Smeralda; the island opens up to tourism.

Mid-1990s Last of the Sardinian mines closed.

2005 Four new Sardinian provinces created: Olbia-Tempio, Ogliastra, Carbonia-Iglesias and Medio-Campidano.

2008 Renato Soru resigns as president of Sardinia. American nuclear submarine base at La Maddalena is shut down.

2009 Soru stands for president; loses to right-wing Ugo Cappellacci.

2013 18 people die as Cyclone Cleopatra hits the island.

2014 Cappellacci is succeeded by Francesco Pigliaru (Democratic Party).

2015 Serving his second term, Italian president Giorgio Napolitano retires and is replaced by Sergio Mattarella.

2019 Right-wing coalition wins Sardinia's local elections.

Cathedral of the Immaculate, Bosa

WHERE TO GO

GETTING AROUND

The island is too large to explore from a single base. If touring, two weeks would be just adequate to sample the different aspects of the coast and the sightseeing highlights, but to see the island comfortably you would need a month. If time is limited to a week or less, make your base in one of the main regions, taking day trips to the coast or forays inland to remote rural areas. The provincial capitals of Cagliari and Sassari are well worth visiting but are not ideal as tourist bases.

CAGLIARI AND THE SOUTHEAST

CAGLIARI

Capital of the island and its main port, **Cagliari** ❶ is the most cosmopolitan and modern of Sardinia's cities. Industrial outskirts and traffic-choked streets can be intimidating, but the heart of the old city retains plenty of picturesque charm and historical interest. Along with churches, monuments and museums the city provides the best choice of restaurants and shops on the island and, to the east, a huge sandy beach and flamingo-filled lagoon.

'Karalis' as it was originally named, was one of several settlements in southern Sardinia established as trading posts by the Phoenicians. By the time of Roman rule, it had become one of the main trading ports of the Mediterranean. The most striking legacy of Roman occupation is the **Anfiteatro** (Amphitheatre; www.beni culturalicagliari.it; May–mid-Oct Fri–Sun 9am–5pm, mid-Oct–Apr Sat–Sun 10am–7pm; guided visits) carved out of the rock on

the hillside in the Stampace quarter of the city. Battles between gladiators and beasts drew audiences of 10,000; today the ruins make an evocative setting for concerts, opera and theatre. The town's earliest example of Christian architecture is the heavily restored **Basilica of San Saturnino** (Tue–Sat 9am, 10am–1pm and 3.30–7.30pm, though often closed) on Piazza San Cosimo, in what is now modern Cagliari. Built to commemorate the Sardinian saint who was martyred on this spot in 303, it is a beautiful domed 5th-century cruciform church with a distinctly oriental look.

The bulwarks of Cagliari's medieval defences were built on the hill by the Pisans, who took control in the 13th century. A ring of walls (best seen from afar) was constructed around the city, followed by two defence towers in 1305 and 1307 built in anticipation of Spanish invasions. Pisan concern was not unfounded and the Aragonese put an end to their rule in 1324. Several centuries of Iberian domination finished ingloriously in 1708 when the city yielded to a small Austro-British naval force without so much as a fight.

Castello

On top of the hill, the Pisan- and Aragonese-built **Castello** Ⓐ was the former political, religious and administrative centre. This is the oldest and most interesting quarter of the city, with its monuments, narrow alleys and picturesquely dilapidated dwellings. It is easily covered on foot, though you can hop on one of the tourist 'trains' that depart from Piazza Carmine for a 45-minute guided tour. By foot it's best to start at Piazza Costituzione, then climb the monumental stairway of the **Bastione San Remy** Ⓑ. The views from the esplanade, where you can sit with a drink, encompass the city, port and lagoons. West of the bastion lies the Pisan-built **Torre dell'Elefante** (Elephant Tower; www.beni-culturalicagliari.it; closed for renovation at the time of writing).

The name derives from the little carved elephant which you can see on a plinth on the Via Università side. The tower took on a grisly role under Spanish rule when the severed heads of prisoners were hung in cages above the portcullis. You can admire the views from the tower (when it reopens) or those from the terrace of the nearby Caffè Libarium Nostrum (Via Santa Croce) on the city walls.

Cattedrale di Cagliari

To the east, Piazza Palazzo is flanked by 18th-century buildings and, in one corner, by the striking **Cattedrale di Cagliari** Ⓒ (www.duomodicagliari.it; Mon–Fri 8am–12pm, 4–8pm, Sat–Sun and holidays 8am–1pm, 4.30–8.30pm). This Pisan Romanesque church was rebuilt in the 17th century and given a mock Romanesque facade in 1938. The multicoloured interior is essentially Baroque but retains marble gems from the original church: the 12th-century pulpits on the entrance wall, exquisitely carved with reliefs illustrating *The Life of Christ*, and, in front of the altar, the four lions, each with their prey. The elaborate crypt (entered via a doorway behind the far-right lion) houses the tombs of the Savoy royal family. Next to the cathedral is the much rehashed Archbishop's Palace, and beside it the Palazzo Viceregio, built by the Aragonese for their viceroys. Today it is home to the provincial assembly and occasionally opens to the public for exhibitions.

Prize exhibits

The Phoenican, Roman and Byzantine periods are all well represented at the Archaeological Museum, but the prize pieces are the Nuragic *bronzetti*, exquisite and often humorous statuettes of humans and animals which would not look out of place in a stylish modern art gallery.

At the far end of the Piazza, the **Torre di San Pancrazio** (San Pancrazio Tower; same hours as Torre dell'Elefante) was built at the highest point of the city to keep guard over vessels sailing through the Gulf of Cagliari. The Aragonese used it as a storehouse and lodging for government officials, and from 1600 it became a prison.

Citadella dei Musei

At the northern end of Castello, the **Citadella dei Musei** ❶ (Citadel of Museums) is an imaginative cultural centre of gardens and modern museums, incorporating the remains of the Spanish Royal Arsenal. If you choose to visit just one museum make it the **Museo Archeologico Nazionale** ❷ (National Museum of Archaeology; www.museoarcheocagliari.beniculturali.it; Wed–Mon 9am–7.30pm), housing treasures from major sites throughout the island. Arranged on four floors, the collection provides an overview of successive cultures from Neolithic to early medieval. The upper floors are arranged topographically, focusing on the main Nuragic and Roman sites in the Cagliari province. A combined ticket gives you entry to the **Pinacoteca Nazionale** (National Art Gallery; www.pinacoteca.cagliari.beniculturali.it; Tue–Sun 8.15am–9.15pm) whose most interesting works are the Quattrocento and Cinquecento altarpieces, many of them Catalan.

On an entirely different theme, the nearby **Museo d'Arte Siamese Stefano Cardu** (Cardu Museum of Siamese Art; www.museicivicicagliari.it; Tue–Sun mid-June–mid-Sept 10am–8pm, mid–Sept–mid-June 10am–6pm) is a collection of oriental porcelain, weapons and precious *objets d'art* bequeathed to the city in 1917 by Stefano Cardu. A contractor of public works, credited with the construction of the Royal Palace in Bangkok, Cordu was a Sardinian who lived in Siam (modern-day Thailand) for 20 years, making his fortune and amassing his treasures.

A bizarre collection of anatomical wax models, including macabre cutaway heads and stomachs, is displayed in the **Museo delle Cere Anatomiche di Clemente Susini** (Clemente Susini Museum of Anatomical Waxwork; http://pacs.unica.it/cere; Tue–Sun 9am–1pm and 4–7pm) near the entrance to the Citadella. This unlikely collection was commissioned in 1801 by Carlo Felice, the viceroy of Sardinia.

Marina and Stampace

In the lower town, below Castello, Marina is a busy quarter of shops and restaurants. A favourite spot for a stroll or drink is **Via Roma**, whose dignified arcades shelter traditional cafés and elegant boutiques. The street runs parallel to the harbour where huge Tirrenia ferries constantly come and go. The network of narrow lanes behind Via Roma teems with trattorias. Via Sardegna has the concentration of eateries, from simple café style

Roman Emperor at Museo Archeologico Nazionale

to fine dining establishments. This is a pleasant quarter for wandering, with churches, small food shops and artisans workshops. **Piazza Yenne** to the north is the hub of the Stampace quarter and the starting point of the Carlo Felice highway (SS131), which cuts right through the island to Porto Torres in the north. The road was named after the king who built it, and whose statue stands in the square. Stampace is a quarter of historic churches, the most famous of which is **Sant'Efisio** (Tue–Sun 9am–12.30pm, 4–8pm) on Via Sant'Efisio. The saint is commemorated every May in one of Sardinia's most spectacular festivals (see page 97).

Poetto

The 6km (4-mile) stretch of sands at Poetto can provide a welcome relief after the sweltering streets of the centre. At the southern end it is not the most peaceful of beaches –facilities include funfairs as well as sunbeds and water sports – and the quality of the beach has not been enhanced by the importation of darker sands. But further north there are still large expanses of unspoilt fine white sands. At night the liveliest spot is Marina Piccola, nestling at the foot of the Sella del Diavolo (Devil's Saddle promontory) at the southern end. Poetto also has the added attraction of a huge colony of flamingoes, along with numerous other waders on the Molentargius marshes behind the beach. The lagoon was formerly used for salt extraction and the name derives from Su Molenti, the donkeys that transported the sacks of salt.

VILLASIMIUS

Cagliari's beaches cannot compare with the beautiful stretches of white sand around Villasimius to the east. The resort is reached by a winding road, which clings to the mountainous coast, giving glimpses of sandy and pebbly bays below. The main resort on the southeast coast, **Villasimius**, has seen a tourist boom in recent years with an increasing number of holiday complexes, hotels and villas. Throughout the summer visitors flock here for the golden sands, gloriously limpid waters and the bustling centre of bars, pizzerias and souvenir shops. Some of the best beaches, accessed by dirt tracks, are unsigned. The main road south ends near the lighthouse on the **Capo Carbonara**, scene of many

Su Boe (ox mask) in Villasimius

a shipwreck over the centuries. A path leads up to the lighthouse for views of the **Isola dei Cavoli**, an offshore island that can be visited on boat trips from the marina at Villasimius.

COSTA REI

The SS18 follows the coast west and north from Villasimius, affording breathtaking views of the coastline and islets. En route for the Costa Rei you can branch off right to the lovely white sandy beaches of Cala Pira and Cala Sinzias (the latter has a couple of campsites and fills up in high season). Further north is the Costa Rei proper, with dazzling expanses of white sand and turquoise waters. Developers have taken advantage of this straight stretch of coast, constructing large villa complexes, but happily these don't impose on the beaches themselves. A particularly lovely stretch is the Spiaggia Piscina Rei, with its spacious white sands.

The main centre for the area is **Muravera**, an unremarkable market town surrounded by citrus orchards. If you are returning to Cagliari, there's a beautiful though tortuous route back along the SS125, cutting through the rugged red-walled gorges of the **Monte dei Sette Fratelli** (Mount of the Seven Brothers). The mountains rise to 1,023m (3,355ft) and are one of the rare haunts of the Sardinian stag *(cervo sardo)*.

THE SOUTHWEST

The Punic-Roman ruins of Nora and the extensive Nuraghe Su Nuraxi can be reached easily from Cagliari. Other highlights are the abandoned mines of Iglesiente, the Costa Verde beaches and the islands of San Pietro and Sant'Antioco.

Maritime Madonna

Just off Isola dei Cavoli, local divers sank a modern statue of the Madonna del Naufrago (Shipwreck Madonna), also known as the Madonna dei Fondali (Our Lady of the Seabed), as a tourist attraction. It lies at a depth of 10m (33ft). On the second Sunday of July, the *Festa della Madonna del Naufrago*, a procession of boats, heads out to the spot where the statue lies, to honour those lost at sea.

PULA AND NORA

An uninspiring route via refineries and salt works takes you south from Cagliari. Despite the industry, many species of wading birds inhabit the Stagno di Santa Gilla marshes. To the south the main centre is **Pula**, a busy little town with a useful tourist office and the small Museo Archeologico Patroni (Tue–Sun summer 9am–8pm, winter 9am–5.30pm) with finds from the nearby archaeological site of **Nora** ❷ (same hours as

Nora sits on the Capo di Pula promontory

museum; combined ticket available; guided tours in Italian). Founded by the Phoenicians, then built over by Carthaginians and Romans, the city is peacefully set on the Capo di Pula promontory, overlooked by a 16th-century Spanish watchtower. Excavations have revealed extensive relics including the Punic Temple of Tanit (goddess of fertility), Roman baths with mosaics and an impressive Roman theatre where performances are staged in July. Overlooking the nearby beach, the chapel of Sant'Efisio is the pilgrimage church of Cagliari's Festival of Sant'Efisio in May (see page 97). **Santa Margherita**, southwest of Pula, was developed in the 1960s as an upmarket resort. Luxury hotels are hidden among gardens and pines, with direct access to the white sands. But for the best beaches and a more beautiful coastline head south to **Chia** ❸ and beyond. The Saracen watchtower on a hillock commands a great vista of the dazzling white sands and dunes stretching towards Capo Spartivento.

COSTA DEL SUD

The corniche road that snakes its way along the **Costa del Sud** ❹ from Capo Spartivento affords a magnificent panorama of sheer cliffs, rugged promontories and turquoise waters. Cala Tuerredda, one of the few beaches along the rocky coast, is a sublime spot for a dip. The road ends at Porto di Teulada; the promontory to the west is a military zone and the beaches at Capo Teulada are accessible only by boat (July–Aug, trips from Porto di Teulada).

ISOLA DI SANT'ANTIOCO

Off the southwest coast, the island of **Sant'Antioco** ❺ has been connected to the mainland by a causeway since Carthaginian times. The Romans built a bridge across the Golfo di Palmas, remains of which you can still see at the far end of the causeway. Ignore the industrial port and head for the historic upper town, signed from the seafront. This ancient town, believed to be the first Phoenician colony in Sardinia, became a thriving port and traded in the locally mined lead, zinc and gold. Originally called Sulcis, a name subsequently given to the whole region, its present-day name commemorates Saint Antiochus, an African slave who was tortured by the Romans, tossed into the sea and washed up on the shores of the island. After converting the local people to Christianity, he was martyred in AD 127 and is buried in the early Christian catacombs of the **Basilica di Sant'Antioco** (Church of Sant'Antioco; Mon–Sat 9am–noon and 3–6pm, Sun 10–11am and 3–6pm; guided tours). These fascinating catacombs were created from former Punic tombs and comprise dark, low-lying chambers with niches, some retaining their skeletons or fragments of frescoes.

For the **Area Archeologica** (www.archeotur.it/santantioco; all sites daily Apr–Sept 9am–8pm, Oct–Mar 9.30am–1pm and 3–6pm unless otherwise stated; charge for each site, combined ticket available) take the Via Castello up from Piazza de Gaspari, passing en route the Piedmontese **Forte Sabando**, the remains of the Punic necropolis (on the right) and the acropolis (on the left). The **tophet** (daily 9am–7pm) is a sacred site for the ashes of babies and infants (see page 48). Clusters of orange funerary urns lie among the rocks – these are mainly reproductions. The **Museo Archeologico** (daily 9am–7pm) houses finds from the ancient city of Sant'Antioco and the Sulcis region as a whole. Retracing your footsteps, it's worth making a small detour to the **Museo Etnografico** at Via Necropoli which focuses on farming, bread- and cheesemaking, and other local traditions.

The **Villaggio Ipogeo**, the subterranean chambers of the Punic or Carthaginian Necropolis beyond the museum can be visited with a (non-English-speaking) guide. These small interconnecting chambers were

Sea silk

In Sant'Antioco's Museum of Ethnography look out for samples of the *pinna nobilis*, the huge mollusc from the lagoons which produce byssus – the tufts of silky filaments by which the molluscs adhere to the rock. Known as *seta del mare* (sea silk) the thread was used to make ties, gloves, shawls and other garments until the 1930s.

inhabited for centuries, the last inhabitants being ejected in the 1960s for reasons of hygiene.

Culture apart, Sant'Antioco is a hilly island, with rocky outcrops and cliffs on the west coast, and accessible beaches on the eastern and southern coasts. **Calasetta**, 10km (6 miles) northwest of Sant'Antioco, has a couple of nearby beaches and a port with a regular ferry service to Carloforte on the island of San Pietro.

ISOLA DI SAN PIETRO

Legend has it that St Peter took refuge on this small, rocky island following a shipwreck, hence the name San Pietro. The first inhabitants were a colony of Ligurians who emigrated here from the Tunisian island of Tabarqa. Descendants of fishermen and coral-gatherers who had settled on the African island in the 16th century, they were bequeathed the island of San Pietro in 1738 by King Carlo Emanuele III of Savoy, who was seeking to repopulate Sardinia. Having been subjected to Saracen raids on Tabarqa, the Ligurians then became victims of a French invasion of San Pietro in 1792 and five years later subjected to Saracen slave raids.

Over two centuries later, the inhabitants of the island still speak a Genoese dialect and the local cuisine (which is some of the best in Sardinia) features Ligurian

The mattanza

Shoals of tuna swim through the waters between San Pietro, Sant'Antioco and Portoscuso in early summer, en route to the Black Sea. Fishermen use a system of nets to channel the tuna into the *camera della morte*, or death chamber. Once the chamber is full, the fish are hauled out of the water and bludgeoned to death. Not a pretty sight, but the *mattanza*, or tuna massacre, inevitably attracts crowds.

and North African special-
ities, as well as more gen-
eral Mediterranean ones.

From the Sardinian main-
land, San Pietro is easily
reached by a 35-minute car
ferry from the small har-
bour of Portovesme on the
southwest coast (roughly
every hour). Leaving behind
the view of belching chim-
neys of nearby Portoscuro,
the ferries ply across to San
Pietro's delightful port of
Carloforte. The waterfront
area, overlooked by pastel-

Marina in Carloforte

washed houses, bustles with fishing boats, ferries and pleasure
craft. The town has a handful of small hotels, a string of sea-
view restaurants and cafés, and pleasant walks along the water-
front. The hub is Piazza Carlo Emanuele III, dominated by a large
statue of the king. The small and attractively laid out **Museo Civico**
(mid-June–mid-Sept Tue–Sun 5–9pm and Thu–Sun 9am–1pm,
mid-Sept–mid-June Tue–Sun 9am–1pm and Thu–Sun 3–9pm),
housed in the Carlo Emanuele III fort, has sections on tuna fish-
ing (including gruesome-looking gaffs and axes used for the *mat-
tanza*), transportation of minerals, and island history.

San Pietro's coast is best seen by boat. A typical half-day tour
of the island takes in grottoes, cliff scenery and otherwise inac-
cessible beaches. There is no coastal road that does the full
circuit of the island, though you can gain access to the main
beaches, as well as Capo Sandalo in the west with its towering
cliffs and rare falcons and the Punta delle Colonne in the south,

Cattedrale di Santa Chiara, Iglesias

named after the rock stacks that rise sheer from the crystalline waters.

IGLESIAS

For the capital of a mining region, **Iglesias ❻** is a surprisingly appealing town. It lies in the centre of the Iglesiente, the mountainous region west of Cagliari renowned for rich mineral deposits. Silver and lead were exploited by Phoenicians, Carthaginians and Romans, after which the mines were abandoned until the 13th century when Ugolino della Cherardesca, the tyrannical Pisan leader who featured in Dante's *Inferno*, founded Iglesias and rekindled the industry. From the mid-19th century onwards the mining activities focused on zinc.

The hub of the town is **Piazza Sella**, a large square where local people relax on tree-shaded benches and boys race on cycles around the statue of Quintino Sella (the minister responsible for reopening the mines). The castle tower off the square is one of the few vestiges of the Pisan-built medieval fortifications. From the Piazza, Corso Matteoti, lined with elegant boutiques, brings you into the Aragonese-built old town. With its medieval (and later) churches, pedestrianised streets and Spanish-style houses with beautiful balconies, this quarter makes for a delightful stroll. The central Piazza Municipio is overlooked by the **Cattedrale di Santa Chiara** (daily 8am–noon, 3–7pm), its simple but striking Romanesque and Gothic facade belying a rich 17th-century interior. The cathedral faces the neoclassical **Municipio** (Town Hall), while the south side of the square is filled with the Bishop's Palace.

TEMPIO DI ANTAS

North of Iglesias, the SS126 winds through the mountains towards the ruins of the Roman **Tempio di Antas** (www.star tuno.it; Temple of Antas; May–Sept daily 9.30am–7.30pm, Oct–Apr Tue–Sun 9.30am–4.30pm). The origins are believed to be Nuragic, though the present-day ruins are those of a Roman temple built over a 3rd-century BC Carthaginian sanctuary. The site was discovered in the 1960s and the remaining columns were re-erected in the portico of the temple chamber. This is a delightfully remote spot with walks along *macchia*-scented footpaths. The nearby **Grotte Su Mannau** (www.sumannau. it; Apr–June daily 9.30am–5.30pm, July–Aug daily 9.30am–6.30pm, Sept–Oct 9.30am–5.30pm, Nov–Mar by appointment only; guided tours), signposted off the SS126, is a series of caves with some spectacular stalagmites and stalactites.

MINING CENTRES

The once-flourishing mining industry has left its mark on the region, with abandoned mine shafts and industrial plants scarring the rugged landscapes. The main mines have been opened as tourist attractions, but except in July and August guided tours are by appointment only. Closest to Iglesias (southwest) is **Monteponi** lead and zinc mine (guided tours of its Galleria Villamarina; reservations required; tel: 0781-491 300, www.igeaspa.it).

On the coast, the main Iglesias beach of Fontanamare is a huge, sweeping stretch of unspoilt sands. The road north follows the contours of the coast, providing a visual feast of sheer cliffs, rocky outcrops and views of the strangely shaped

Scoglio Pan di Zucchero (Sugarloaf Rock) jutting out of the sea. Abandoned mines can be seen at Nebida and at Porto Flavia at Masua where ore was loaded onto cargo ships. **Buggeru** was one of the main mining centres, founded in the mid-18th century. Formerly it was only accessible by boat; now it's a seaside resort, with sandy beaches, a port for pleasure craft and the prominent remains of the mines. (For guided tours of the Galleria Henry: tel: 0781-491 300, www.igeaspa.it.) The loveliest beaches in the region are **Cala Domestica** to the south, at the end of an inlet, and **Spiaggia Portixeddu** to the north, a huge expanse of sands, backed by towering dunes.

COSTA VERDE

The **Costa Verde** ➐, north of Capo Pecora, remains remarkably unspoilt by tourism. The name (Green Coast) alludes to the *macchia* that carpets the dunes and rocks. The beaches here are stunning, but the best have to be accessed by twisting mountain roads and/or dirt tracks. The legendary **Piscinas** ➑ beach has 9km (5 miles) of sands, with huge dunes rising up to 50m (160ft). The only development along this remote, desert-like landscape is the chic **Hotel Le Dune**, converted from an old mine building. A dirt track north of Spiaggia Piscinas follows the coast to the small beach resorts of **Porto Maga** and **Marina di Arbus**. The last resort before Oristano province is **Torre dei Corsari**, an untidy sort of place, but graced by a beautiful beach backed by dunes. Inland from Piscinas the mine shafts and buildings in and around the hill town of **Montevecchio** are a legacy of its once-thriving industry. Guided tours in

Visiting the mines

For information on visiting all the mines, tel: 0781-491 300, or go to www.igeaspa.it. All require advance reservations.

The vast nuraghe ruins at Su Nuraxi

English (tel: 070-973 173; www.minieramontevecchio.it; times vary) take in the miners' houses, hospital and church, and an exhibition on the life of the mining community.

Crowning a nearby hill at Villanovaforru is the **Nuraghe di Genna Maria** (www.gennamaria.it; Tue–Sun 9.30am–1pm and 3.30–6pm or 7pm, depending on season), whose main attraction is the 360-degree panorama, which, weather permitting, encompasses almost half the island. But if your interest is purely archaeological, skip this one and head for Sardinia's oldest and most extensive nuraghe ruins: **Su Nuraxi ❾** at Barumini (daily summer 9am–7pm, winter 9am–5pm ; guided tours every 30 minutes).Tours, normally in Italian only, are compulsory, and queues are possible in summer, though you can get quite a good view of the central section from the roadside. The imposing central tower is only two-thirds of its original height with only two of the three storeys still intact. Built around 1500 BC, it

was later fortified by ramparts and corner towers which still stand. A village developed around the fortifications with about 200 circular dwellings, some of which have been reconstructed. The decline came with the Carthaginian invasion of the 6th century BC, although the site was partially reconstructed and inhabited until Roman times. The complex as a whole is best seen from the top of the central tower – from here, too, you have good views of a ruined 12th-century castle crowning a remarkably conical hill to the south.

In the centre of Barumini the **Casa Zapata** (www.fondazione barumini.it; daily 10am–5pm; combined ticket available with Su Nuraxi) was built in the late 16th century as the noble residence of the Spanish Zapata family. Excavations in 1990 (which are still ongoing) revealed that the palazzo had been built over an ancient Nuragic site, foundations of which can now be viewed along the walkways above. The museum also has a history section relating to the Zapata dynasty, archaeological finds from the Su Nuraxi nuraghe and an ethnography section.

ORISTANO AND THE WEST

The least known of Sardinia's provinces, Oristano has no international airport (the nearest are Cagliari and Alghero) and the

region is largely ignored by tourists. The coast is one of cliffs, rocky promontories and long, deserted stretches of beach. Major cultural highlights are the ancient city of Tharros and the Sinis Peninsula, the well-preserved Nuragic complexes of Losa and Santa Catarina and the centre of the provincial capital, Oristano.

ORISTANO

When the once-flourishing port of Tharros was finally defeated by Saracen raids in the 11th century, the inhabitants moved inland and resettled at the small village of **Oristano ⑩**. It became the capital of the Giudicato of Arborea (one of Sardinia's four autonomous territories) and in the 14th century flourished under the rule of the warrior, Eleonora of Arborea. Following her death in 1404 the region fell into decline and today only vestiges survive of the medieval fortifications.

Oristano is the capital of the province and the only main town of western Sardinia. The dignified town centre is well worth a visit, particularly the 19th-century **Piazza Eleonora**, presided over by

⊙ WILD HORSES OF GIARA DI GÉSTURI

This extensive plateau north of Barumini is home to abundant wildlife, and in particular famous for *cavallini* – the small wild horses, distinguished by their dark manes and almond-shaped eyes. The species has been protected since the 1960s and the number roaming on the plain has risen to around 700. You are most likely to see them at the ponds known as *paulis* – apart from the summer months when the water evaporates. To reach the plateau, follow the Altopiano signs from Gésturi. A tourist office provides information on the plateau and printed details (in English) on the various footpaths, both botanical and archaeological.

Bell tower of Cattedrale di Santa Maria

a large statue of the town's heroine; the elegant **Corso Umberto**, and the town's main museum. The city walls were demolished long ago and the only remaining medieval fortifications are the **Torre di San Mariano II** (also called Torre di San Cristoforo) in Piazza Roma and the nearby Portixedda (Little Tower). The other main landmark of the centre is the beautiful onion-domed octagonal bell tower of the **Cattedrale di Santa Maria** (Apr–Oct Mon–Sat 8.30am–noon and 4–7.30pm, Sun 8am–1pm, Nov–Mar 8am–1pm and 3–6.30pm; free) on Piazza Mannu. The church was built in 1228 but underwent a major Baroque revamp in the 17th century. If your next stop after Oristano is the ancient city of Tharros, don't miss the **Antiquarium Arborense** (www.antiquariumarborense.it; Mon–Fri 9am–8pm, Sat–Sun 9am–2pm, 3–8pm) in the Palazzo Parpaglia on Piazza Corrias. This excellent archaeological museum displays a collection of finds from Tharros and the Sinis Peninsula: Nuragic ceramics and tools, Phoenician jugs, weapons and jewellery, Punic pottery and Roman amphorae, glassware and gemstones. The small art gallery focuses on 15th- and 16th-century altarpieces, which show a marked Catalan influence.

On a hillock 3km (2 miles) south of the city, the **Basilica di Santa Giusta** is a beautiful example of the Pisan Romanesque style. A former cathedral that would have enjoyed uninterrupted views of the lagoon prior to Santa Giusta's modern development, it is a lofty three-naved church with granite and marble columns plundered from Tharros and the nearby Roman city of Neapolis. The frescoed Renaissance chapels were added in the 16th century, and the campanile in 1875 to replace the old one that collapsed.

THE SINIS PENINSULA

Northwest of Oristano the **Sinis Peninsula** ⑪ is a low-lying area of white-sand beaches, marshes and lagoons full of flamingoes. **Cabras** is the main town, set on a large lagoon (the Stagno di Cabras) which is the source of the mullet offered in various forms in the many local fish restaurants. The **Museo Cívico Giovanni Marogiu** (www.museocabras.it; daily Apr–Oct Mon–Sat 9am–1pm and 4–8pm, Sun 9am–1pm and 3–8pm, Nov–Mar Tue–Sun 9am–1pm and 3–7pm) on the banks of the lagoon displays treasures salvaged from Tharros, and the prehistoric site at Cuccuru in Arrius, 3km (2 miles) southwest of Cabras. The ethnographical section features samples of the traditional *fassonis*, flat-bottomed fishing boats made of rushes and formerly used on the lagoons.

The deserted village of **San Salvatore**, west of Cabras, featured in several Spaghetti Westerns in the 1960s. The only event that wakes the village these days is the Festival of San Salvatore in late August and early September. Pilgrims who come to celebrate the nine-day event stay in the huddle of little houses or *cumbessias*. The fascinating church of San Salvatore (hours vary, church run by volunteers) originated around a Nuragic sanctuary, which was constructed over a sacred well. Inside, steps lead down to the subterranean chambers where you can see an altar dedicated to Mars and Venus, and fragments of wall frescoes, drawings and graffiti dating back to Punic, Roman, Arab and Spanish times.

Just before Tharros, the **Church of San Giovanni di Sinis** is, with San Saturnino in Cagliari, the oldest Christian monument

Detail inside the Church of San Giovanni di Sinis

in Sardinia. It was originally built in the 5th century and, though much restored, retains its Greek cross form and Byzantine style. The church fell into ruins in the 1820s and was used as a shelter for shepherds and animals.

The ancient city of **Tharros** ⑫ (daily 9am–5pm) was founded by the Phoenicians around 730 BC at the southern tip of the Sinis Peninsula. Under the Carthaginians it became one of the most important trading ports of the western Mediterranean. The Romans improved the city with streets, baths and an aqueduct, but from the 7th century Saracen raids marked the fate of the city and by 1070 it had fallen into decline. Two-thirds of the site is submerged under water, due to subsidence, but excavations have revealed substantial Roman and, to a lesser extent, Punic remains. Dominating the ruins on the eastern slope, and rising theatrically above the sea are two white columns from a Roman temple. Other relics, including a cistern, forum, thermal baths and small temple are not so easily identifiable, and it's worth taking a guide if one is available. To the north the Carthaginians built a *tophet* and an acropolis on the hill, over the remains of a large Nuragic settlement.

If you're looking to cool off after exploring the ruins, the nearby beach of San Giovanni di Sinis is more sheltered than those north of Tharros and less crowded than Oristano's main beach, Marina

di Torre Grande. The beaches to the north, often pounded by huge rollers, afford some spectacular scenery. **Is Arutas** ⑬ is one of the loveliest, composed of grains of shiny white quartz and washed by crystal-clear waters. Further north the resort of Putzu Idu is a departure point for boat trips to the **Isola di Mal di Ventre**, 10km (6 miles) offshore. Commonly mistranslated as Stomach Ache Island, the name actually derives from *Malu Entu* or evil wind, after the strong mistral that blows for most of the year. The longest and most exposed of the beaches is **Is Arenas** which has 6km (4 miles) of undeveloped sands backed by dense

◎ SA SARTIGLIA

Oristano is at its liveliest between the last Sunday of Carnival and Shrove Tuesday when it hosts the famous Sa Sartiglia festival (www.sartiglia.info). This flamboyant three-day affair is rooted in pagan rituals guaranteeing the return of spring. Weeks ahead of the festival two kings (or Componidori) are chosen for their equestrian expertise; one is the king of the Guild of Farmers, the other of the Guild of Carpenters. The main event is the Corso dell'Anello joust when the horsemen, and especially the Componidori, clad in masks and medieval costumes, charge down a long, wide track lunging their spears at a small star-shaped ring suspended on a rope. The more rings that are lanced, especially by the Componidori, the better the chance for the oncoming harvest. In the final ride, the Componidori lies down face-up on his horse, blessing the audience with periwinkles and violets. The Corso dell'Anello is followed by La Pariglia, with participants performing extraordinary equestrian feats. On the following day children take part in a mini Sa Sartiglia, riding *cavallini*, the little horses from the Giara di Gésturi (see page 45).

woods of pine and acacia. To the north the picturesque resort of **S'Archittu** is named after a natural limestone arch where locals leap into the beautiful clear waters of the inlet.

A dirt track off the main road leads to the ruins of **Cornus**, site of the last revolt of the Carthaginian and Sardinian forces against Roman rule in 216 BC. Saracen raids in the 10th century forced the inhabitants to desert the town and set up inland – at present-day **Cuglieri**. On the western slopes of Monte Ferru, the village can be spotted from afar by the silver dome of the Basilica di Santa Maria della Neve.

THE INTERIOR

The dominant feature of northern Oristano is **Monte Ferru** (Iron Mountain), an ancient volcanic mass formed of trachyte and basalt. Forests of oak and sweet chestnut flourish on the mountain slopes; lower down, particularly around Seneghe, the olive groves are said to produce some of the best olive oil in Italy. The main village is **Santa Lussurgiu**, set inside the crater on the eastern slopes. The traditional pursuits of the region, including leather work, carpentry, weaving and wine-making are displayed in the Museo della Tecnologia Contadina (tel: 0783-550 617; www.museotecnologiacontadina.it; by appointment only) on Via Deodato Meloni. From the village a scenic mountain road takes you to San Leonardo di Siete Fuentes, renowned for its mineral waters.

SANTA CRISTINA AND NURAGHE LOSA

Northeast of Oristano, and easily accessible from the SS131 highway to Sassari, are two of Sardinia's major archaeological sites. **Santa Cristina** ⑭ (daily 8.30am–8.30pm, off-season 9.30am–6pm), lying among olive groves, was a major Nuragic settlement. Excavations revealed extensive remains including dwellings, a 15m (50ft) high tower and, most significant of all, a well-temple in a remarkably good state of preservation, dating possibly from the 1st millennium BC. The **Church of Santa Cristina** was built on the site in c.1200, and the huts you see around it, known as *muristenes*, are used by pilgrims who come to worship during the Santa Cristina festival days – the only time the church is open. Finds from the well-temple can be seen in the Museo Archeologico-Etnografico (Tue–Sun 9am–1pm and 4.30–7.30pm in summer, 3–5.30pm in autumn–winter, 3.30–6.30pm in spring) in the Palazzo Atzori in **Paulilatino**, 5km (3 miles) northeast of Santa Cristina.

⊙ PUNIC TOPHETS

Although ancient Greek historians described *tophets* as Punic sites where infants were cruelly sacrificed to the gods, modern-day archaeologists believe they were sanctuaries for the ashes of stillborn babies or deceased infants. Cremation rituals often entailed the sacrifice of small animals; the ashes were then placed in an urn beside a sacred stone decorated with symbolic figures of gods. These Punic sites date from the 5th to the 3rd century BC.

Nuraghe Losa

Continue heading along the SS131 for the **Nuraghe Losa** ⑮ (www.nuraghelosa. net; daily 9am–one hour before sunset). The focal point here is a massive keep dating back to 1500 BC. This is surrounded by ramparts, minor towers and outer walls, all of which were added at a later date. You can gain access to the nuraghe through a narrow passageway to see the vaulted chambers and, from the terrace (depending on the weather) the peaks of the Gennargentu mountains.

East of Nuraghe Losa, Ghilarza's main claim to fame is as the birthplace of Antonio Gramsci, one of the founders of the Italian Communist Party in 1921. The town is now home to the Casa di Gramsci museum and study centre (www.casa-gramscighilarza.org; Wed–Mon 10am–1pm and 3.30–6.30pm). Gramsci links apart, Ghilarza is an uninspiring sort of place.

South of Ghilarza, **Fordongianus** – or Forum Traiani as it was originally called – was founded by the Romans after the discovery of hot springs. Impressive remains of the baths, the **Terme Romane** (daily summer 9.30am–1pm and 3.30–7pm, off-season 2.30–5pm) can be seen on the banks of the River Tirso, where the main stream gushes out at a temperature of 54°C (130°F). The steaming waters here are still occasionally used for washing clothes by local women (who claim the results are superior to those of modern washing machines). Fordongianus is distinctive for the red trachyte stone used in the churches and houses and the modern outdoor sculpture for which it is renowned. The most notable house is the late 16th-century **Casa Aragonese** (daily 9am–1pm and 3–6.30pm in summer, 5.30pm in winter) in the centre, a restored Catalan noble's dwelling which preserves its porticoed entrance and decorated Gothic-Aragonese doorways and windows.

South of Oristano, **Arborea** was founded in 1928 as the main focus of Benito Mussolini's agricultural development scheme. The River Tirso was dammed, a huge expanse of marshland drained and scores of new farms established for settlers from northern Italy. It is still a rich and fertile region.

NUORO AND THE EAST

The province of Nuoro covers the mountainous heart of Sardinia, a region of wild landscapes and remote villages and towns. Notorious for banditry, Nuoro has not traditionally endeared itself to travellers. Today, however, the interior is opening up to trekkers, climbers, spelaeologists – or those just curious to see Sardinia at its most Sard. The region stretches to the eastern coastline, fringed by enticing bays and pristine waters.

NUORO

The location of **Nuoro** ⑯, the provincial capital, on a great granite plateau facing the rocky heights of the Supramonte, is its most striking aspect. The town itself has limited tourist appeal, lacking picturesque charm and surrounded by modern sprawl, but it's pleasantly uncommercialised and has some interesting literary links and an excellent ethnographical museum. The **Corso Garibaldi**, the main shopping street, cuts through the old town and leads into the central Piazza San Giovanni. Off the Corso on Via Sebastiano Satta, the **Museo**

*Mask on display in Nuoro's
Museum of Sardinian Life*

d'Arte Nuoro or **MAN** (Museum of Nuorese Art; www.museoman.it; Tue–Sun 10am–8pm) is a stylish setting for temporary exhibitions and a permanent collection of works of art by leading 19th- to 21st-century Sardinian artists. In Via Mannu the **Museo Archeologico Nazionale** (Tue–Sun 9am–7.15pm) has a small but impressive collection of local archaeological finds, ranging from neolithic to medieval. More popular, however, is the **Museo Etnografico della Sardegna** (www.isresardegna.it; mid-Mar–Sept Tue 5.30–7.30pm, Wed 10am–1pm and 5.30–7.30pm, Thur 11am–1pm and 5.30–7.30pm, Fri 10am–noon and 5.30–7.30pm, Sat 5–8pm, Sun 10am–1pm and 5–8pm; Oct–mid-Mar daily 10am–1pm and 3–5pm), on the southern edge of town at Via Antonio Mereu 56. The collection gives an excellent insight into local traditions, crafts and festivals. Exhibits include some exquisite costumes and textiles, jewellery, weapons, musical instruments and, most striking of all, sinister figures with black wooden masks, sheepskin clothing and strings of cow bells dangling on their backs. During local carnivals similarly clad figures perform ritual dances, culminating in a symbolic 'killing' of the scapegoat.

Nuoro is renowned as the birthplace of leading Sardinian *literati*, among them the prolific Grazia Deledda (1871–1936), winner of the Nobel Prize for Literature in 1926. Although she married young and moved to Russia, her 50 or so novels are set in her native Nuoro and portray the passions of its people. The author's house in Via Grazia Deledda, tucked away in the atmospheric Santu Predu quarter, is now the **Museo Deleddiano** (www.isresardegna.it; Tue–Sun mid-Mar–Sept 10am–1pm and 3–7pm, Oct–mid-Mar 10am–1pm and 3–5pm) devoted to Deleddiano memorabilia (in Italian only). Nuoro was also home to Sardinia's most famous poet, Sebastiano Satta. Small bronze statues of the poet can be seen in the **Piazza Sebastiano Satta** where he lived.

From Nuoro you can see the village of **Oliena** across the valley, dominated by the slopes of Monte Corrasi. The setting is dramatic but there is not a lot to detain you in the grey stone centre. The town is mainly used as a launching pad for hiking and climbing in the **Supramonte di Oliena**. The old quarter is the most compelling part of town and, with its impossibly narrow sloping streets, is best explored on foot. The Oliena region is known for its excellent Cannonau wine.

⊙ BANDITRY IN THE BARBAGIA

The scene of kidnapping and violence in the 1950s and 1960s, Orgosolo earned itself the reputation as the capital of banditry. The violence, rooted in feuds between local shepherds and farmers, was immortalised in Vittorio De Seta's award-winning film, *Banditi a Orgosolo* (Bandits at Orgosolo) in 1961. From 1960–9 there were 414 murders and countless kidnappings on the island, mainly by shepherds in the Barbagia region. But Orgosolo had long been a centre of vendettas. From 1901–54 there was on average a murder in the village every two months.

One of the many murals in Orgosolo

ORGOSOLO

South of Oliena, **Orgosolo** ⑰, the 'bandit capital of Sardinia', lies deep in the wild Sopramonte mountains. The setting is dramatic and there is a certain fascination about its notorious past, but Orgosolo is an unpretty town, fringed by dreary apartment blocks. Signs are peppered with bullet holes and the many **murals**, immortalising the vendettas, add to the slightly sinister feel of the place. The first murals appeared in the 1960s and were followed by scenes depicting political or social themes. Today there are more than 150, many of them vibrant and accomplished works of art. Some recent additions depict 9/11 and the toppling of Saddam Hussein.

If you happen to be in the region in mid-January or at carnival time in February head straight for **Mamoiada** west of Orgosolo. The town is famous for its masked festivities (see page 97) and has a **Museo delle Maschere** (Mask Museum; www.museodellemaschere.it; daily 9am–1pm and 3–7pm) in Piazza Europa. Hand-crafted masks are also sold locally.

THE GENNARGENTU NATIONAL PARK

The Barbagia centres on the Gennargentu, a great granite massif whose name, Silver Gate, derives from the shimmering effect of the sun on the snowy slopes. This wild and remote region covers 59,000 hectares (146,000 acres), and, at **Punta La Marmora** rises to 1,834m (6,015ft), the highest peak in Sardinia. From here views encompass almost the entire island. The granite mountain peaks are barren but the lower slopes are carpeted in forests of oak and chestnut. In winter, skiers take to the slopes of Bruncu Spina near **Fonni**, which at 1,000m (3,280ft) is the highest town in Sardinia. Further south, the village of **Aritzo**, amid forests of sweet chestnut, is pleasantly refreshing in summer and enjoys fine views of the mountains. In former times the village sold chests of snow throughout the island, and you can see the straw-lined boxes used to transport it in the **Museo della Montagna** (Mountain Museum; Tue–Sun June–Sept 10am–6pm and 4–7pm, Oct–May 9am–1pm and 3–6pm).

EAST COAST

Gloriously unspoilt beaches are the main draw of Nuoro's east coast. In the north, along the Costa degli Oleandi (Oleander Coast), **Posada** is a gem of a village, huddled below the tower of its ruined medieval **Castello della Fava** (Bean Castle; daily summer 9am–1pm and 3–6pm, off-season until one hour before sunset). Posada flourished as a military stronghold in medieval times, but pirate attacks and malaria took their toll. The hilltop tower and ruined walls command sweeping views of the sea, river and fertile plain. The village lies inland from a huge stretch of undeveloped but exposed beach.

OROSEI

Orosei is the capital of the Baronia region, dominated on the western side by the long barren ridge of Monte Albo. Land here was reclaimed after the eradication of malaria and today the fertile plains are planted with citrus orchards, olive groves and vineyards. A flourishing coastal port in late medieval times, the town was forced inland by the silting up of the River Cedrino. It is one of Nuoro's more appealing towns, with a lively central square, some fine churches and excellent beaches nearby. The town's heart is the **Piazza del Popolo**, overlooked by the **Cattedrale di San Giacomo**. The showpiece of Orosei, the cathedral has a fine tower and five tiled cupolas, though is rather spoilt by the neoclassical facade added at a later date. Nearby, Piazza Sas Animas is flanked by the Chiesa delle Anime and the remains of the grim-looking castle which became the Prigione Vecchia (Old Prison). The town's oldest church, though much restored, is the 15th-century Chiesa di Sant'Antonio on the eponymous piazza.

DORGALI AND THE GOLFO DI OROSEI

The road south from Orosei twists down to **Dorgali**, a town on the southern fringes of the Baronia, overlooking valleys of vineyards and olive trees. About 8km (5 miles) before the town a road branches off to the **Grotta di Ispinigoli** (www.ghivine.com/Ispinigoli.htm; Ispinigoli Cave; daily tours on the hour July–Aug 9am–7pm, Apr–June and Sept–Oct 9am–noon and 3–6pm, Nov–Mar noon and 3pm). This huge chamber was discovered in the 1950s by shepherds sheltering from a storm. The findings of Phoenician jewellery and the bones of a 10-year-old-girl suggest the cave was used for human sacrifice. *Ispinigoli* or 'thorn of the grotto' refers to the 38m (125ft) stalagmite, claimed to be the largest in Europe and the second

Bidderosa beach

The Orosei coast is fringed by beaches, marshes and pines. The loveliest beach here is Bidderosa, edging the protected Bidderosa Park. The number of visitors and cars is restricted and in high season you are asked to purchase a pass from the forest station of Bidderosa on the SS125 at the park entrance (tel: 333-179 8335; May–Oct daily 8am–7.30pm).

largest in the world. This striking column links the floor to the vault – the top metre is in fact a stalactite, while 37m (121ft) have grown from the ground, a process that has taken around four million years.

Dorgali is a major centre of handicrafts, particularly leather, hand-woven carpets, embroidered shawls, ceramics and gold filigree. Occasionally you can see craftsmen at work, throwing a pot or creating haversack-

Pretty but busy Cala Luna

like leather 'shepherds' bags'. The region is liberally endowed with archaeological sites, caves and canyons; the tourist office on Via Lamarmora can supply you with details of the many guided trips – you can choose from jeep, foot, kayak, bus, bike or horse.

Three kilometres (2 miles) south of Dorgali, the road to the coast corkscrews through terraced vineyards and oak trees, then plunges under the limestone rock before emerging at the glistening sea of **Cala Gonone**. Tucked below the mountains, this is the only real resort on the **Golfo di Orosei** ⑱ to the south, a ravishing coastline of limestone cliffs and pristine beaches, lapped by waters of every imaginable shade of blue and green. This 20km (12-mile) stretch is inaccessible by car, and the port of Cala Gonone does a roaring summer trade in boat excursions – sea shuttle, sailing boats or motor cruises. Alternatively you can hire your own motorised dinghy (no experience required). The cliffs are riddled with deep grottoes, the most renowned

The Costa Smeralda, a popular destination for the jet-set

of which is the **Grotta del Bue Marino ⑲** (Grotto of the Sea Ox; guided tours). This spectacular cave, full of weird and wonderful shapes, is named after the rare monk seal which used to breed here. After the cave was opened to the public (in the 1940s) the seals gradually began to disappear. The next beach down is **Cala Luna ⑳**, a sublime spot (until the boatloads arrive) with towering cliffs, caves, *macchia*-covered rocks and oleanders. Another beauty spot is Cala Sisine, the next beach on; but the real gems are further south at **Cala Mariolu** and **Cala di Goloritzè**.

On a volcanic plain 11km (7 miles) northwest of Dorgali, **Serra Orrios** (July–Aug 9am–1pm and 4–7pm, Oct–Mar and Apr–June 9am–1pm and 2–5pm, Sept 9am–1pm and 3–6pm; guided tours only) was one of the largest Nuragic settlements on the island. It spreads over 6,000 sq m (7,200 sq yds) and may have accommodated 600–700 villagers. A hundred huts have been discovered, along with two temples.

West of Dorgali, **Su Gologone** has two claims to fame: the Sorgente Su Gologone, which is the largest spring in Sardinia, and the charming Su Gologone Hotel with a restaurant renowned throughout the island for delicious Barbagia cuisine (see page 138). Su Gologone is also the starting point for the highly recommended hike to Valle Lanaittu and **Monte Tìscali**. In the late 19th century woodcutters discovered the remains of a Nuragic village, concealed at the foot of a huge cave within the mountain itself. The dwellings were squat and tower-like with walls of limestone blocks and roofs of juniper wood. Today only traces remain, but excavations continue. From the Valle di Lanaitto, where you must leave the car, it's a 1.5–2-hour, relatively strenuous, hike up the mountain. Provided you're reasonably fit you could try doing the walk alone. The path is waymarked by red triangles for most of the route, but a guide is recommended (ask at the tourist office in Oliena or Dorgali). South of Tiscali the Su Gorroppu canyon (see page 92) offers some spectacular hiking, preferably with a guide.

COSTA SMERALDA AND THE NORTHEAST

The city of Olbia is the gateway to the Costa Smeralda, a small stretch of wild coastline that has been transformed into an exclusive holiday area for the rich and famous. Beyond it lies Palau, launching pad for the lovely islands of the Maddalena Archipelago, and further north the popular resort of Santa Teresa Gallura, surrounded by enticing beaches. The granite coastline, with its wind-carved rocks, is a dramatic feature of this northeastern corner of the island.

OLBIA

The development of the Costa Smeralda led to the creation of an international airport at Olbia. Since tourism took off

here, the population has trebled (it is the third largest town in Sardinia), and the ferry port, being closest to the mainland, is the busiest on the island. Visitors arriving at its airport justifiably ignore the town centre and head straight for the resorts. It is one of the oldest cities in Sardinia, but only traces survive from its Punic, Roman and medieval past. The only worthwhile monument is the **Basilica di San Simplicio** (Basilica of San Simplicio; 8am–1pm and 4–7pm), an unadorned Pisan Romanesque granite basilica behind the railway station.

The Gulf of Olbia is dominated by the great bulk of the **Isola Tavolara** ㉑, an uninhabited island with sandy beaches, a tiny harbour and a couple of trattorias. Summer ferries depart from the busy beach resort of Porto San Paolo south of Olbia and there are boat excursions stopping off here and at the smaller neighbouring Isola di Molara (Island of Molara).

COSTA SMERALDA

North of Olbia the summer traffic crawls to the **Costa Smeralda** ㉒. Roads branch off east to **Golfo d'Aranci** (Gulf of

⊙ THE COSTA SMERALDA

The story goes that when the Aga Khan sailed past this small strip of remote coast in 1958 he decided it would make the perfect holiday spot. Four years later, heading a private consortium, he bought the land from local farmers. The coastline of rocky capes, sheltered coves and ravishing sandy bays was to become the most famous holiday playground in the Mediterranean. Today the hotels and bars command some of the highest prices in Europe – the Hotel Cala di Volpe is so exclusive that in high season you need celebrity status to stay there.

Crabs, not Oranges), a busy port and villa resort, and, on the peninsula to the west, the **Porto Rotondo** (Round Port). The resort doesn't quite make it geographically into the Costa Smeralda, but certainly competes, with a swish marina, chi-chi boutiques and Silvio Berlusconi's 27-room holiday villa.

Although the name is often used to refer to the whole area between Olbia and Palau or even Santa

Porto Cervo resort

Teresa Gallura, the Costa Smeralda is limited to the stretch between Cala di Petra Ruja, on the Gulf of Cugnana, and Liscia di Vacca, in the north. When the Costa was created strict rules were laid down: a limited amount of land was to be built upon, nothing was to be high-rise or garish, the building stone was to conform to strict specifications, any trees and plants uprooted by construction were to be replaced and all newly planted vegetation was to be indigenous to Sardinia. The regulations were adhered to and building was limited to villas and villa-style hotels, sprouting discreetly amid luxuriant gardens; **Porto Cervo**, the only resort, was created to accommodate luxurious pleasure craft and provide Milan-style boutiques and people-watching cafés. It is all undeniably tasteful though, it has to be said, somewhat contrived and prohibitively expensive.

La Piazzetta in the centre of Porto Cervo is the place to watch the fashion parade go by, preferably in the early evening.

Across the beach the huge, exclusive yachting marina is one of the best equipped in the Mediterranean.

The Costa is liberally endowed with four- and five-star hotels, most with private beaches reserved for guests. For others, beach space is at a premium. Signposting is poor and in high season you may have to park some distance away. Among the loveliest **beaches** are Poltu di li Cogghj (also called Il Principe), Cappricioli and Liscia Rujas. Liscia di Vacca in the north has brilliant white sand, accessed via a dirt track. Beyond here, resorts become, relatively speaking, cheaper and livelier.

ARZACHENA

The inland town of **Arzachena** ㉓, set amid rolling hills and vineyards, is the main centre for the Costa Smeralda. The old centre is more Sardinian than anything you will see on the coast, particularly on market day (Wednesday) when colourful stalls spill on to the streets. Hidden in the rural surroundings of the town are the remains of some **Nuragic tombs and temples** (tel: 0789-81066; Easter–Oct 9am–sunset, Nov–Easter call for an appointment; cumulative tickets and guided tours available in English).

The five sites are not easy to locate, but you can pick up a map from the tourist office 3km (2 miles) east of the town on the Olbia road. The **Nuraghe Albucciu** is easily accessed across the road (via an underpass) from the tourist office; the **Tempietto Malchittu** is a 2km (1.5-mile) walk from the office, along an idyllic country path; the small roofless temple below a mysterious rocky outcrop is thought to date from the early Nuragic period (1500–1200 BC). To the west **Coddu 'Ecchju** (also known as Coddu Vecchiu), and **Li Lolghi** are striking examples of 'giants' tombs' (see page 15). At **Li Muri**, on a country road near Li Lolghi, the circles of stones mark the site of a major necropolis dated 3500–2700 BC.

PALAU

Returning to the coast, **Palau** is a lively resort and ferry port, linked in summer to Naples, Genoa and Porto Vecchio in Corsica and all year round to the nearby islands of the Maddalena Archipelago. The stiff breezes are ideal for yachting, and **Porto Pollo** (also known as Portu Puddu), 7km (4.5 miles) to the west, is a haven for windsurfers. The coastline around here is studded with remarkable wind-sculpted rock formations, including the famous **Roccia d'Orso**, a huge bear-shaped rock 6km (4 miles) east of the town, near the Capo d'Orso fort. A symbol of Palau, the bear has served as a landmark for sailors since ancient times.

West of Palau on the Porto Rafael road, the austere-looking **Fortezza di Monte Altura** (daily June–Aug 10.15am–1pm and 5–8pm, Apr–May 9am–noon and 5–6pm, Sept–mid-Oct 10am–noon and 3–6pm; guided tours) was built in the 19th century to defend the coast, although it was never actually put to the test. The obligatory tours are in Italian only, but the main attraction is really the superb view of the Maddalena Archipelago.

ARCIPELAGO DELLA MADDALENA

According to Nelson, the anchorage between mainland Sardinia and the archipelago was 'the finest man o'war harbour in Europe'. His fleet was frequently present here in the

run up to Trafalgar and he tried, unsuccessfully, to persuade the British to purchase Sardinia (they opted for Malta instead).

The archipelago consists of seven main islands and over 50 islets. In 1994 the whole area was designated a national park to safeguard the environment. The main **Isola della Maddalena** ㉔ is just 20 minutes by ferry from Palau and is hugely popular in summer. The arrival point is the little fishing port of **La Maddalena** – a lively town, with plenty of cafés and bars to quench the thirst of the sailors at the naval base (although their presence has been much reduced since the closure of the nearby US naval base in 2008). West of town, the **Museo Archeologico Navale Nino Lamboglia** (www.sardegnacultura.it; tel: 0789-790 633; Mon–Sat 9.30am–12.30pm and 3.30–6.30pm; by appointment) exhibits treasures from shipwrecks, including amphoras, bronze figures and jewels recovered from a Roman vessel that capsized by the island of Spargi around AD 120.

The sparsely inhabited island of **Caprera**, linked to La Maddalena by a causeway, is principally visited for the **Compendio Garibaldi** (www.compendiogaribaldino.it; Mon & Sun 8.30am-1.15pm, Tue–Sat 8.30am–1.15pm and 1.45-6.45pm), the last home of the great Italian unification leader. Garibaldi (1807–82) purchased part of the island, built a home, and managed to use the infertile terrain for farming, vegetable growing and viticulture. Guided tours (usually in Italian) of the Casa Bianca (White House) take in Garibaldi memorabilia including his famous red shirt, his deathbed (the clocks are fixed at the time of his death) and the tomb where he was buried in 1882.

The other main islands, Budelli, Razzoli, Spargi and Santa Maria, can be visited only by boat. Excursions from La Maddalena (or Palau) stop off at secluded beaches. The beguiling waters are ideal for scuba diving or snorkelling and the islands are a paradise for private yachts. One of the loveliest beaches is Budelli's beautiful **Spiagga Rosa**, famed for the enchanting pink-tinged sands. To protect the beach, swimming here is forbidden. The two little islands to the north, Isola Razzoli and Isola Santa Maria, are separated by the Passo degli Asinelli, named after the donkeys that used to carry provisions from Santa Maria to the lighthouse at Razzoli.

◉ THE CORK OF GALLURA

You won't have to drive far in Gallura to spot the cork oak. The tree (*Quercus suber*) is easily recognised by its twisted branches, glossy green evergreen leaves or the raw red trunk where the bark has been recently stripped. Cultivating the cork is a lengthy process. The trees must mature for 25–30 years before the first cutting of the outer layer. Skilled foresters strip off the roll of bark using special axes, leaving the tender inner layer undamaged. The bark grows again but is not ready for restripping for another nine or 10 years. The process is repeated and the quality of the cork improves year by year. The virgin cork is fit only for floors, floats, life-jackets or decorative purposes: the superior cork in champagne or wine bottles will be from the second or subsequent strippings.

SANTA TERESA GALLURA

The northern tip of Sardinia is buffeted by the *mistrale*, resulting in strange rock formations. The most spectacular is **Capo Testa** ㉕, a promontory of white granite boulders west of Santa Teresa Gallura. From the lighthouse you can walk to scenic coves, including Cala dei Corsari where Roman columns can be seen on the sea bed. The promontory, which is joined to the mainland by an isthmus lined with beaches, was once a quarry, and the granite was used for Rome's Pantheon and Pisa's cathedral.

The nearby resort of Santa Teresa looks across to Corsica, 11km (7 miles) away. The town of Bonifacio makes a popular day trip – ferries make the crossing several times daily (fewer off-season). Ferries also link the resort with La Maddalena. The oldest part of Santa Teresa dates from the early 1800s when King Vittorio Emanuele repopulated it with Piedmontese and named it after his wife, Teresa. The town expanded into a holiday resort in the 1960s. Off-season it is quiet, but come June and July the streets teem with tourists. The centre is lively, with bars, trattorias and street markets. A fine 16th-century Spanish watchtower stands on the promontory between the port and the beach. The central beach, Spiaggia di Rena Bianca, is

Climbing over Capo Testa

packed in summer, but beaches on the Capo Testa isthmus are less busy, as are the lovely white sands to the east.

TEMPIO PAUSANIA

From Palau the *Trenino Verde* (the little green train, see page 133) climbs up to **Tempio Pausania**, in the wooded heart of Gallura. Far removed from the summer bustle on the coast, the region's capital lies high in the hills, with clear mountain air, therapeutic springs and dignified streets lined with grey granite houses. South of Tempio, the mountain range of Monte Limbara rises to 1,359m (4,457ft) and its peak, **Punta Balistrieri**, affords sweeping vistas.

From Tempio, a road snakes up to **Aggius**, an attractive village strikingly set among granite outcrops. The impressive **Museo Etnografico Oliva Carta Cannas** (MEOC; www.museodiaggius. it; daily May–mid-Oct daily 10am–1pm and 3–7pm, mid-Oct–Dec and Feb–Apr Tue–Sun10am–1pm and 3.30–7.30pm) is devoted to local crafts and industries, ranging from breadmaking and carpet-weaving to granite quarrying and cork production. Apart from its industry, Aggius is renowned for a long-standing vendetta between two families, which resulted in 72 murders.

ALGHERO AND THE NORTHWEST

The northwest has a host of attractions, from the charming old quarter of Alghero and the historic towns of Bosa and Castelsardo to the Pisan Romanesque churches, prehistoric nuraghe and stunning sands of Stintino.

ALGHERO

Tradition has it that the Emperor Charles V, on a visit to **Alghero** ㉖ in 1541, found the city *bonita y ben asentada* – charming and well located. Over four and a half centuries later,

the description still holds true. It is arguably the most appeal-ing of Sardinia's tourist centres, with a picturesque medieval core and a coast of white beaches and glorious azure waters.

Set on the northwest coast, the town faces the Iberian Peninsula, which played such a major role in its history. In 1353 the Aragonese overthrew the Genoese who had founded a fortress here in the early Middle Ages; the local Sardinians and Ligurians fled, and the town was repopulated with Catalans. Alghero became part of the Kingdom of Aragon and remained in Spanish hands for four centuries. It still retains Spanish characteristics, in the architecture of its monuments, the Catalan street names (alongside Italian ones), the archaic form of the Catalan language still spoken here and the Catalan-style seafood dishes served in many restaurants.

The population of 45,000 more than doubles in summer and visitor numbers continue to rise with the boom in cheap flights to Fertilia airport. But tourism has not spoiled Alghero's charm. It is a fishing port as well as a tourist centre, and unlike most Sardinian resorts, stays alive all year.

The city can easily be covered on foot and the pedestrianised streets of the centre make are pleasant. The beautifully preserved **Centro Storico** (Historic Centre) comprises a network of narrow cobbled alleys, flanked by mellow stone houses. The Catalan architectural influence can be seen in some of the carved portals and windows with Gothic arches. The perimeter of the old town is marked on three sides by the old city walls and the sturdy towers embedded in them. At sunset the sea-facing *bastioni* or ramparts on Bastioni Marco Polo are the place for the *passeggiata* (evening stroll). But at any time of day a walk along the walls affords wonderful views.

Via Carlo Alberto is the busiest and most elegant of the main arteries, lined by small shops selling crafts, clothes and coral jewellery. The **Chiesa di San Francesco** (Church of St Francisco; daily 9am–noon and 5–7.30pm) is a notable landmark with a Gothic campanile and attractive cloister (accessed via the

○ WHAT'S IN A NAME?

Scholars are divided on the derivation of the name Alghero. The original name was S'Alighera and the most accredited hypothesis (though not the most popular locally) is that it comes from the Latin algae, or seaweed – which off-season still invades the shores. The name could also come from the Arabic *Al Gar* meaning cave, alluding to the Grotta di Nettuno (Neptune's Cave). The name *S'Alighera* was later changed to *Algarium*, and then by the Aragonese to the Catalan *L'Alguer* – the name still used in local dialect.

sacristy) where concerts are held in summer. At the end of the street the multicoloured majolica-tiled dome of the Church of San Michele is a conspicuous landmark and symbol of Alghero. The **Cattedrale di Santa Maria** (Mon–Tue and Thu–Sat, June–Aug 10.30am–1pm, 7–9.30pm, Apr–May and Sept–Oct 10.30am–1pm, 4–6.30pm) on Piazza Duomo is a hodgepodge of styles. An ostentatious, neoclassical facade belies a Renaissance interior with Baroque chapels and an elaborate carved altarpiece and pulpit. The beautiful Catalan-Gothic bell tower (guided tours June–Aug 10.30am–1pm and 7–9.30pm, Apr–May and Sept–Oct 10.30am–1pm and 4–6.30pm), with a fine sculpted portal, is easily missed in Via Principe Umberto behind the church.

RIVIERA DEL CORALLO AND GROTTA DI NETTUNO

The **Riviera del Corallo**, west of Alghero, is named after the coral reefs at the foot of the limestone cliffs. The finest beaches, Le Bombarde and Lazzaretto, lie beyond Fertilia, the soulless town created by the Fascists in 1936 as part of a large land-reclamation programme. The bay of **Porto Conte**, where some of Alghero's smartest hotels hide among the pines, is a large natural harbour fringed with sandy bays. The panoramic coast road takes you south to **Capo Caccia**, the imposing limestone promontory formerly used for game shooting and today a haunt of the herring gull and (more rarely) the peregrine falcon. Just before the tip of the promontory a road leads to the Escala del Cabirol, a dramatic stairway of 656 steps

Boat to the grotto

A less strenuous way of reaching the Grotta di Nettuno is by excursion boat from Alghero. You can either take a *traghetti navisarda* (tel: 079-950 603; www.navisarda.it), a sailing boat (luxurious) or waterbus (cheapest and most comfortable when the sea is choppy).

descending 110m (360ft) to the entrance of the **Grotta di Nettuno** ㉗ (Neptune's Grotto; daily Apr–Oct 9am–7pm, Nov–Mar 10am–3pm; guided tours), the most spectacular of Sardinia's caves. Since the first mention of this fairy-tale cavern in the 18th century, writers and travellers have extolled its virtues. One of them, English barrister, John Tyndale, likened it to the Alhambra. In the 19th century, sailors used to illumi-nate the cave with hundreds of candles and at one time it was the setting for candlelit concerts (today it's lit by electricity).

The Grotta di Nettuno

ARCHAEOLOGICAL SITES

Roughly halfway between Alghero and Capo Caccia, a layby provides an excellent view of the **Nuraghe di Palmavera** (daily Apr–Oct 9am–7pm, Nov–Feb 10am–2pm, Mar 9.30am–4pm), a fortified Nuragic village which was abandoned in the 5th century BC. The remains comprise the principal and original limestone tower (1500–900 BC), the secondary tower, ramparts and 'Meeting Hut' (900–800 BC), and 50 or so circular dwellings, added in the final phase (800–700 BC). To the north, on the Alghero–Porto Torres road, the **Necropoli di Anghelu Ruju** (same hours as Nuraghe di Palmavera; combined ticket available) is an extensive complex of 36 burial chambers, known as *domus de janas* (fairy houses), dating from the late Neolithic era (3300–2900 BC). The size of some

of the tombs suggests collective burials and the finds, including female idols, bowls and deposits of shells, mixed with ash and charcoal, are evidence of funerary rituals and feasts.

Near the necropolis is the smart **Sella and Mosca** wine estate, surrounded by lush gardens and 500 hectares (1,235 acres) of vineyards. They produce a whole range of wines, and free guided tours (www.sellaemosca.it; June–Oct Mon–Fri 5.30pm, also Sat in high season) take in the cellars, museum and a film on the estate's history. The Enoteca (wine shop) is open all year.

BOSA

South of Alghero, the coastal road curves along the wild rocky shore and cuts through hills carpeted in clumps of gorse and euphorbia – a spectacular riot of yellow in late spring. Near Capo Maragiu watch out for griffon vultures circling above – this is home to the largest colony in Italy of these rare birds.

In the Remo River valley, surrounded by mountains, **Bosa ❷⓼** feels quite remote. The **Castello Malaspina di Fosdinovo** (tel: 0187-680013; www.castellodi fosdinovo.it; guided tours on the hour: May–Sept Wed–Mon 11am–noon and 4–6pm, Oct–Apr Sat 3–5pm, Sun 11am–noon and 3–5pm) towers above the town and is evidence of

Bosa and the River Temo

Bosa's importance in medieval times. It was built on the hill as a fortress in the 12th century, though only the walls and towers survive. Within the castle the little 14th–15th-century Church of Nostra Signora di Regnos

Malvasia di Bosa

Look out for the rich, amber-coloured Malvasia di Bosa, sold in wine cellars and shops, and served in all Bosa's restaurants.

Altos shelters a remarkable 14th-century cycle of frescoes. The castle ramparts command fine views of the mountains, sea and town. Huddled below is the old town of **Sa Costa**, a maze of alleys and picturesque, tumbledown houses. On the left bank of the Temo lie the abandoned tanning buildings of **Sas Conzas** quarter. Bosa was famous for cowhide and throughout the 18th century had a thriving trade with Genoa and France. Nineteenth-century travellers who praised the beauty of Bosa invariably mentioned the foul smells of the tanneries and river, emanating from the mixture of water and dog excrement used to purge the skins and give them greater elasticity.

The **Cattedrale di San Pietro Extramuros** (Apr–Oct Tue–Sat 9.30am–12.30pm, Apr–June also Sun 3.30–6.30pm, July–Aug also Sat 4–6pm and Sun 6–7pm, Sept–Oct also Sun 3–5pm), Bosa's former cathedral, lies 2km (1.5 miles) upstream. Formerly part of a Cistercian monastery, it is a simple and evocative Romanesque church with a Gothic facade. The present-day counterpart is the **Cattedrale dell'Immacolata**, a rococo-style church on the Corso Vittorio Emanuele II. This main thoroughfare running through the centre was home to the wealthy bourgeoisie and is lined by elegant houses, such as the **Casa Deriu** at No. 59 (Tue–Sun 10.30am–1pm and 6–11.30pm, off-season by appointment). Small cavernous shops occupy the lower floors of some of the houses.

SASSARI

Sassari ㉙ is the principal city of northern Sardinia and the second largest on the island. Despite being a busy commercial centre, surrounded by unsightly swathes of industry, it's an attractive place to observe Sardinian town life. It also has an old quarter of medieval streets and the second best archaeological museum on the island. Sassari developed as a medieval town when Saracen raids on the coast forced the inhabitants to retreat. Pisan rulers were followed by Catalan Aragonese, who controlled the city for four centuries. In the 16th century the Jesuits established Sardinia's first university here, and the city is regarded as the island's intellectual capital. It is also famous for its festivals: the **Cavalcata Sarda**, featuring an equestrian parade and frenzied horse racing and the **Festa dei Candelieri** when huge wooden candles are borne in procession along Corso Vittorio Emanuele II.

The town's hub is **Piazza d'Italia** Ⓐ, a spacious, stately square, with central, palm-shaded gardens. The east side is flanked by the neoclassical Palazzo della Provincia (Town Hall). In the early evening Sassaresi can be seen en masse strolling in the piazza or taking aperitifs at one of the bars under the colonnades on the northwest side of the square. To the north of Piazza d'Italia is Piazza Castello, where recent archaeological excavations have revealed two Barbican passageways which are now open to the public (guided tours: Tue 10am–1pm, Wed–Sat 10am–1pm and 4.30–7.30pm, Sun 10am–1pm).

Going up from Piazza d'Italia, the Via Roma is home to Sassari's most elegant shops, as well as a useful tourist office and, at No. 64, the **Museo Nazionale G. A. Sanna** Ⓑ (www. musei.sardegna.beniculturali.it; daily Tue–Sun 9am–8pm; first Sun of each month free). The impressive collection ranges from the Neolithic to the Roman, and encompasses Phoenician

Duomo di San Nicola, Sassari

and Carthaginian finds. An extensive Nuragic section displays reconstructions of sanctuaries and some superb bronzes.

In the heart of the old town, the **Duomo di San Nicola** Ⓒ rears up from a small square, the extravagant Spanish Baroque facade fronting an otherwise Gothic structure. It's worth exploring the *vincoli* (alleys) around the church with their cavernous stores, local restaurants and occasional artisan workshops. On the other side of Corso Vittorio Emanuele II, there is a daily morning market in pretty little **Piazza Tola**.

BASILICA DELLA SANTISSIMA TRINITÀ DI SACCARGIA

The **Basilica della Santissima Trinità di Saccargia** ㉚ (www. arcidiocesisassari.it; Apr–Oct daily 9am–6pm), Sardinia's most famous Romanesque church makes quite an impact as you hurtle along the Sassari–Olbia highway. In a valley 16km (10 miles) southeast of the city, it has an eye-catching black

and white striped facade and a soaring bell tower. Built by the Pisans in the 11th century, it once formed part of a large monastic complex. *Saccargia* means dappled cow in Sardinian dialect – the valley was pastureland and there are depictions of cows among sculpted decorations in the porch. The interior is simple and evocative, and the central apse is enhanced by the only existing cycle of 13th-century frescoes in Sardinia.

The Saccargia church is just one of the Pisan Romanesque jewels in the region, all easily reached from the SS597: the abandoned **San Michele di Salvenero**, 3km (2 miles) south-east of the Saccargia church; the brown and black basalt **Santa Maria del Regno**, dominating the hilltop village of Ardara, with a huge and elaborate early 16th-century *retablo* over the altar; and the beautiful **Sant'Antioco di Bisarcio** near Ozieri – once a cathedral, now completely isolated.

OZIERI

The town has lent its name to the Ozieri Culture, dating from 4th and 3rd millennia BC when the first villages were established on the island. Finds from this era, including ceramics and statuettes, were discovered in the Grotta di San Michele on the outskirts of Ozieri and can be seen in the small **Museo Archeologico** (Tue–Fri 9am–1pm and 3–7pm, Sat–Sun 10am–1pm and 3–6pm) in the ex-convent of Clarisse on Piazza Petro Micca. The grotto itself is also open to the public but is of limited interest. Little survives of old Ozieri, but it has a fine setting, its houses and apartments stacked up on the valley slopes.

VALLE DEI NURAGHI

The region southwest of Ozieri, strewn with the remains of ancient civilisations, has been dubbed the 'Valley of the

Nuraghi'. If you only have time for one of them, make it **Nuraghe Santu Antine** ㉛ (www.nuraghe santuantine.it; daily 9am–8pm; guided tours), about 4km (2.5 miles) south of Torralba and easy to get to from the main SS131. The nuraghe was built and inhabited between the 15th and 9th centuries BC. The oldest section is the massive central keep, at 17.5m (57ft) – originally it was around 22m (72ft)

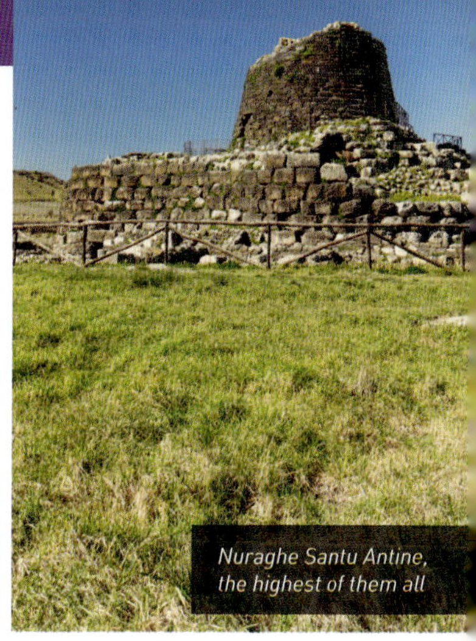
Nuraghe Santu Antine, the highest of them all

with a third storey. The tower is surrounded by a three-sided rampart, incorporating three secondary towers. Scant remains of Nuragic, Carthaginian and Roman villages lie outside the walls. Torralba's museum contains finds from the site and a small-scale model of the nuraghe.

NORTH COAST

Porto Torres, or Turris Libisonis when it was a Roman colony, was founded by the Romans in 27 BC and became a major trading centre with temples, thermal baths, basilicas and splendid villas. Today it is essentially an industrial ferry port, whose oil refineries, petrochemical works and unsightly outskirts deter all but the most dedicated sightseers. The **Basilica di San Gavino** (www.basilicasangavino.it; Apr–Oct daily 9am–1pm and 3–6pm) is a beautiful example of Pisan Romanesque architecture and the largest church of its type in Sardinia, although

swamped by modern development. The church is dedicated to saints Gavino, Proto and Gianuario who were beheaded in AD 304 for converting to Christianity. They are commemorated by wooden statues in the church and sarcophagi with their remains in the lower crypt. The church's Roman marble columns suggest there was a temple on or near the site.

Near the railway station, just back from the seafront, the **Antiquarium Turritano** (Thur–Tue 9am–6pm) testifies to the importance of the former Roman colony. Visits start with the excellent archaeological museum, housing Roman finds, and continue to the archaeological site known as Palazzo del Re Barbaro, the palace of the Roman governor Barbarus. The site includes remains of the public baths, mosaic floors, roads and shops.

Between Sassari and Porte Torres, and marked off the main SS131, the sanctuary of **Monte d'Accoddi** (Apr–Sept Tue–Sat 9am–6pm, Sun 9am–2pm, Oct–Mar Tue–Sat 9am–5pm, Sun 9am–2pm) is a rare sacred mound left by the pre-Nuragic Ozieri Culture. The high pyramidal mound, flattened at the top, is surrounded by high walls of limestone blocks and has a ramp leading up to what was some form of altar or shrine.

STINTINO

On a narrow windswept peninsula at the northwest tip of Sardinia, **Stintino** was formerly no more than a peaceful fishing village. It still is off season, but in summer tourists pour in for the beautiful beaches, seafood restaurants and the hotels and villas that have sprouted up. The village was founded by 45 families of fishermen and farmers who were exiled from neighbouring **Asinara** in 1885 when the latter was turned into a penal colony and quarantine station. The prison closed in 1994 and today the 17km (10-mile) windswept island is an uninhabited national park, with unpolluted beaches, mouflons (long-horned wild sheep) and white donkeys *(asini)*, after which the island is named. From Easter to September excursions to the island depart from Stintino and Porto Torres (numbers limited to 500 a day; for information on boats and excursion 'trains' see www.treninoasinara.it).

In Stintino's picturesque old port, lateen sailing boats sit side by side with fishing boats and pleasure craft. The prime attraction is the **Pelosa beach** ❷, 4km (2.5 miles) to the north, a Caribbean-like expanse of fine white sands, lapped by blue-green waters. Offshore a ruined Aragonese watchtower dominates the island of Piana – with Isola Asinara beyond.

Stintino used to be a major tuna fishing centre, renowned for the annual *mattanza* or tuna massacre (see page 38).

A mural depicting Stintino's mattanza

Near the new port, the **Museo della Tonnara** (June–mid-Sept 6–11pm) demonstrates through film, video and marine memorabilia the methods of netting and killing the fish. The practice was abandoned in 1974, by which time the tuna migration routes had changed and the high-cost traditional fishing rituals could no longer compete with new techniques.

CASTELSARDO

The SS200 follows the coast east of Porto Torres to **Castelsardo** ㉝, a fortress village that perches picturesquely on a high rocky promontory. Over the centuries the name has been changed according to the colonisers: from the early 12th century, when the Genoese established a castle here, it was Castel Genovese, from the mid-15th

Former sleepy fishing village Stintino

century Castel Aragonese, and since the mid-18th century (when Sardinia became part of the House of Savoy), Castelsardo. The heavily renovated castle was inhabited by the illustrious Dorian family, and is thought to have been the home of Eleonora of Arborea and her Genoese husband, Brancaleone Doria, for around 10 years.

> **Elephant Rock**
>
> The famous and much-photographed Roccia dell'Elefante (Elephant Rock) stands 4km (2.5 miles) southeast of Castelsardo, at the intersection of the SS200 and SS134. The wind-sculpted elephant hides the ancient remains of rock-cut tombs known as *domus de janas*.

The castle terraces command splendid sea views, stretching as far as Corsica on a clear day. The castle houses the **Museo dell'Intreccio** (Museum of Basket-weaving; Apr–Oct daily 9.30am–1pm and 3pm–midnight, Nov–Mar Tue–Sun 9.30–1pm and 3–5.30pm). Castelsardo is a long-established centre for basketry made from dwarf palm leaves, reeds and asphodel. Basket-weaving was formerly the occupation of almost every female in town, from young girls to grandmothers.

The town retains its charm despite large numbers of tourists. Tightly packed houses and small shops selling handicrafts and souvenirs cluster at the foot of the fortress, and women weaving baskets can sometimes be seen in the doorways of tiny alleys. The **Cattedrale di Sant'Antonio Abate**, conspicuous by its fine majolica-tiled cupola, perches precariously on the rocks. The altar is graced by a 15th-century painting of *Madonna con gli Angeli* (Madonna with Angels), by the Maestro di Castelsardo – a much-admired Spanish-influenced artist about whom little is known.

In local costume at a festival

WHAT TO DO

ENTERTAINMENT

NIGHTLIFE

For action after dark you should head for the late-night bars or clubs *(discoteche)* in the capital, other main towns or the more lively coastal resorts where discos in summer are open until the early hours of the morning. The town of Alghero is quite lively by night, with open-air bars in the historic centre and clubs in summer down by the seafront. In Cagliari the stylish bars on Bastione San Remy are the place to be for cocktails and live music at weekends. For information on clubs, discos, theatre and concerts consult the local newspapers, *La Nuova Sardegna* (http://lanuovasardegna.gelocal. it) and *L'Unione Sarda* (www.unionesarda.it), which have sections in English in summer; or visit the tourist office.

THEATRE AND MUSIC

Cagliari's Anfiteatro Romano is a dramatic setting for drama, music and dance performances. Rock concerts are held at the Fiera Campionaria east of the city. In high season ancient sites such as Tharros and Noro host theatre, opera and concert performances. Movie aficionados will find cinemas in the main towns, but films are rarely in their original language.

SHOPPING

The island has seen a revival in traditional handicrafts. Some of the craft work is beautifully made, decorated with designs based on Punic and even earlier symbolic patterns. Along with authentic crafts come the inevitable kitsch and imitation goods, from mock coral to fake Gucci bags sold by hawkers on piazzas and beaches. (Note that fines of up to €10,000 are imposed on shoppers caught buying counterfeit goods.) To see the genuine Sardinian article head for the Ente Bilaterale Artigianato Sardegna at Via Goceano 8 in Cagliari or Tutto Artigianato at Via Roma 50 in Castelsardo. If you like intricately patterned fabrics and carpets, Tessuti Sardi at Via Sarrabus in Muravera is a must-visit. You can sometimes buy direct from the source, particularly in villages where local people display their home-made crafts.

ANTIQUES AND CURIOS

An antiques and curio market is held in Cagliari's Piazza del Carmine on the third Sunday of the month, and a flea market is held in Piazza Trento on every Sunday morning and on the Bastione St Remy (Oct–May every Sunday morning, June–Sept Wed–Sun 6.30pm–midnight). Handmade shepherds' knives, both antique and modern, are widely sold; those with hand-carved horn handles are the most valuable. The main knife-making centre is the village of Pattada in the province of Sassari, and the knives are known as *pattades*. Other popular souvenirs are replicas of little bronze Nuragic figures.

Myrtle liqueur

A favourite souvenir of Sardinia is a cork-wrapped bottle of *liquore di mirto*, distilled from the berries of myrtle plants that proliferate on hillsides.

BASKETWARE

Basket-making is a centuries-old craft. In the Campidano area local women still make baskets from dwarf palm leaves and rush, which are then decorated with strips of red cloth to create traditional

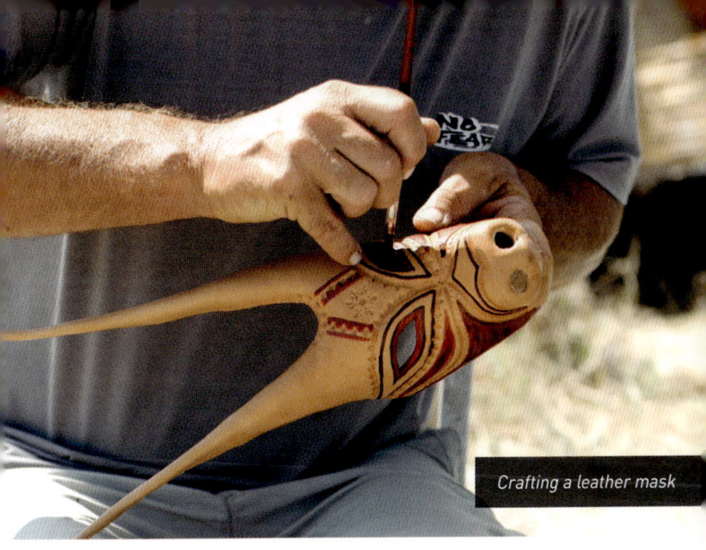

Crafting a leather mask

designs. In the province of Nuoro, asphodel is used to make mats and baskets. In Castelsardo you can still see women weaving baskets on the steps of their houses in the streets of the old town. Samples of locally made basketware, from food containers to lobster pots, can be seen in the Basket-weaving Museum in Castelsardo's castle (see page 83).

CLOTHES AND ACCESSORIES

For Italian designer ware, Sardinian towns can't compare with the mainland, but Cagliari has some smart boutiques and, for those with well-lined wallets, the Costa Smeralda has an abundance of designer labels and chic jewellers. In Cagliari, try Via Manno, between Bastione di San Remy and Piazza Yenne, and Largo Carlo Felice. Via Roma, facing the waterfront, has some elegant boutiques and is also home to La Rinascente, the island's main department store, selling high-quality clothes

A stall selling the local flatbread speciality, carta di musica

and accessories (www.rina scente.it; Mon–Sat 9am–9pm, Sun 10am–9pm). In Alghero the main shopping street is Via Carlo Alberto, where there are clothes and jewellery shops.

FOOD AND WINE

Look out for signs on the road side for cheeses, hams, smoked meats, olive oil, honey or liqueurs. *Agriturismi* (rural properties offering accommodation) often sell home-made produce. Cagliari's Marina quarter (the streets behind the main Via Roma) have specialist food shops with a wide selection of pecorino and other cheeses, as well as wild boar ham, smoked meats, sea urchin pâté, local wines and spirits. Sapori di Sardegna at Vico dei Mille 1 (www.saporid-isardegna.com) and Via Baylle 6 (Via Roma) offers the whole range of Sardinian specialities: *bottarga* (dried mullet roe) from Cabras, *carta di musica* (flat crisp Sardinian bread), piquant *pecorino* cheeses, wines and *filu e ferru* (the local firewater).

The Mercato Coperto di San Benedetto at Via Cocco Ortu (Mon–Sat 7am–2pm) is the longest indoor market in Italy, with a wonderful array of fish, cheeses, hams and other regional specialities.

In Alghero, Dolce e Piccante at Vicolo Buragna 4 stocks the best Sardinian wines along with salamis, cheeses and *dolci*. If you're killing time before a flight home from Alghero's Fertilia airport, drop in to the nearby Enoteca (wine shop) at the Sella

and Mosca Estate (see page 74) for a wide range of wines. In the Barbagia region, Tonara is renowned for *torrone*, a type of nougat sold throughout the island.

JEWELLERY

Delicate gold and silver filigree, as worn with traditional Sardinian costumes, is made by local jewellers; this is often combined with coral to make earrings, necklaces, bracelets and rings. Alghero's streets have numerous coral shops, although little of it comes from the depleted reefs on its Riviera del Corallo.

TEXTILES AND CERAMICS

The best buys are handwoven carpets, rugs and wall hangings, often decorated with geometrical patterns, cotton tablecloths, embroidery, linen and lace. Dorgali in Nuoro province is a major centre for handicrafts, particularly for carpets, embroidered shawls, ceramics, jewellery and leather. Specific to the region are the large triangular 'shepherds' bags' sold in leather shops. Ceramics, sold all over the island, range from traditional ter-racotta ware to innovative modern vases and bowls.

CHILDREN'S SARDINIA

Italians are indulgent towards children and Sardinians are no exception. They will always be made to feel welcome, and are readily accepted in restaurants. Although there are few attrac-tions specifically designed for youngsters, the island offers sandy, gently shelving beaches with idyllic seas for swimming and a wide range of water sports. Most families opt for a resort and stay put, deterred by the long distances (often along hair-pin bends) between main towns and resorts. The majority of coastal hotels have their own pools with a separate paddling

section for youngsters. Some of the larger establishments lay on entertainment for children of all ages.

BEACHES AND BOAT TRIPS

Main beaches have water sports facilities as well as pedaloes, canoes and banana boats. For a change of scenery try one of the boat excursions. Popular trips are the Maddalena Archipelago, either on a day's organised excursion or by ferry from Palau; the island of Tavorola east of Olbia; and the pristine beaches on Nuoro's east coast, accessible by boat from Cala Gonone.

SIGHTSEEING

Unless your child is a budding archaeologist, interest in the pre-historic Nuragic stone cones and archaeological museums is bound to wane after a while. More appealing are hilltop castles, grottoes and catacombs. Of the main towns, Alghero has the most to offer: car-free alleys, seafront walks, medieval towers, a lively port and exciting boat trips to the Grotta di Nettuno. The

⊙ FUN PARKS

Aquadream water park at Baia Sardinia (tel: 0789-99511; www.aquadream.it; mid-June–mid-Sept 10.30am–6 or 7pm) offers swimming pools, chutes and other aquatic activities. Water Paradise north of Sorso in Sassari province, off the Porto Torres–Castelsardo road (tel: 331-1477-670; www.waterparadise.it; June–Sept 10am–7pm) has similar facilities. At Sardinia in Miniature in Tuili (tel: 37-135-7035; www.sardegnainminiatura.it; daily 9am–7pm) you can stroll through all the island's main monuments. The village is close to Barumini and a trip could be combined with Su Nuraxi.

Aquarium, though not spectacular, has more than 100 species of fish.

SPORTS

With 1,800km (1,125 miles) of coastline and clear blue waters, Sardinia is ideal for all types of water sports. The offshore winds make it a haven for sailing and windsurfing, and the sea is ideal for swimming and scuba diving. Recent years have seen a surge in other outdoor pursuits, from hiking and biking to kayaking and caving. *Agriturismi* (rural holiday accommodation) often provide opportunities for exploring the countryside, on horseback, by bike or on foot.

Sardinia is ideal for families

CYCLING

Hiring a bike is a great way of exploring the island, though the hills and mountains make for some strenuous pedalling. Mountain-bike holidays, in groups or on self-guided tours, are becoming increasingly popular. Overnight stays are often in local *agriturismi*. For information, contact Dolce Vita Bike Tours (www.dolcevitabiketours.com). Most of the large towns and coastal resorts hire out mountain bikes. Tourist offices can provide details of bike rental locations, along with recommended cycling routes (www.sardegnaturismo.it). There is also a national automated bike-sharing system which also operates in Sardinia in Cagliari, Carbonia and Olbia. The first half-hour

is free of charge, the second half costs €0.50 and subsequent hours €1. For more information visit www.bicincitta.com

GOLF

The most prestigious golf courses on the island are the Pevero Golf Club (18 holes) at Cala di Volpe, Costa Smeralda, tel: 0789-958 046, www.golfclubpevero.it; and the Is Molas Golf Club (18 holes) at Santa Margherita di Pula, Cagliari, tel: 0709-241 006, www.ismolas.it. The third 18-hole course is the Is Arenas Golf and Country Club on the west coast, www.isarenas.it, tel: 0335 125 8322. There are nine-hole courses at Sassari, San Teodoro, Mirana and Villasimius.

HIKING AND CLIMBING

Sardinia has some stunning walking country, especially the Supramonte in the Barbagia region and the Gennargentu mountains. But hiking in the interior is a relatively recent pursuit, and facilities are limited. More tracks are being created, but don't expect a neat network of established and marked paths. Many hikers hire the services of a local guide. Local tourist offices can provide details, or you can find information from the *Associazione Italiana Guide Ambientali Escursionistiche* at www.aigae.org, or the Sardinian branch of the Italian Touring Club, Alpino Italiani CAI (www.cai.it). Heavy shoes are recommended, along with thick socks to give you protection from the thorny *macchia*. Experienced walkers will enjoy the wild Su Gorroppu gorge in the Supramonte. The trail takes two days and requires

Skiing Sardinia

Sardinia has one ski resort at Fonni in the Gennargentu mountains. At 1,000m, (3,280ft) it's the island's highest village, but there is no guarantee of snow.

special equipment for the vertical walls of the gorge. More demanding still is the Selvaggio Blue Route, a stunning coastal route from Cala Luna to Santa Maria Navarrese, involving rock climbing and abseiling.

HORSE RIDING

Horses are very much part of Sardinia's culture, and several of the island's festivals preserve traditions of jousting and horse racing. Dozens of equestrian centres have sprouted on the island, especially near Cagliari, and in the provinces of Oristano and Nuoro. Schools offer riding lessons for all levels, as well as excursions either along the coast or through forests, farms and mountains. The leading equestrian centre is at the Horse Country complex (www.horse country.it), on the coast at Arborea in the province of Oristano.

Rock-climbing with a sea view

SAILING

Wind conditions off Sardinia are ideal for sailing, whether it's a hired dinghy from a local beach or a private yacht cruising the Costa Smeralda. Inexperienced sailors should beware of variable winds and strong currents along the coast. The island hosts major sailing events such as the Loro Piana superyacht regatta in Porto Cervo and the Maxi Yacht Rolex Cup. Numerous ports, marinas and landings are dotted around the Sardinian coast, but permission is usually required for mooring. The

best-equipped and most exclusive port is Porto Cervo on the Costa Smeralda. *Gommoni* (rubber dinghies) can be rented from many of the beaches, and those with cash to spare can charter motorboats or sailing boats, with or without crew. Alternatively, there are plenty of boat excursions from the coastal resorts.

SCUBA DIVING AND SNORKELLING

The great clarity of the water and the numerous coves and grottoes are favourable for scuba diving and snorkelling. The island provides excellent facilities for divers of all standards and there are dozens of diving centres, many of them located on the north and northwest coast. The Alghero region alone has around 20 centres; other popular areas are Stintino on the northwest tip of the island, the Arcipelago della Maddalena in the north, the Golfo di Orosei on the east coast and the Isola di San Pietro in the southwest. Diving centres offer a whole range of possibilities, from a single dive off the sea-shore to day trips, night dives, underwater photography trips and excursions to shipwrecks.

SWIMMING

Sardinia's crystalline waters and pristine beaches offer some of the best swimming in the Mediterranean. Easily accessible beaches are inevitably packed in July and August; at other times of year you can usually find towel space if you are prepared to drive along (unsigned) dirt tracks, hire a boat or go for a long hike. Hotels frequently have their own beach facilities, but rarely include them in the room rate.

WINDSURFING

Windsurfing is hugely popular in Sardinia and the conditions are perfect, especially on the bays of the north coast. Boards can be hired on the majority of beaches and many hotels will supply them. The most favourable spots in the north are La Maddalena, Santa Teresa di Gallura, Porto Pollo west of Palau and La Pelosa north of Stintino; in the south popular spots are the island of Sant'Antioco, Capo Spartivento and Poetto beach near Cagliari.

Windsurfing near Cagliari

FESTIVALS AND SEASONAL EVENTS

Virtually every village and town finds an excuse for a festival and more than a thousand are celebrated every year on the island. It may be a *sagre*, a religious celebration in honour of a saint, a pagan ritual celebrating the season, or one of the major events that draw participants from all corners of the island. Whatever the occasion the wine flows and the food is abundant. For the main festivals local people dress in exquisitely embroidered costumes and take part in major parades; some of the best-known ones involve feats of horsemanship and frenetic Palio-like races. But there are also less formal, rural festivals, focusing perhaps on some small country church where locals participate in a service, tuck into a huge meal at trestle tables, then dance off the calories to the accompaniment of an accordion.

Opposite is a list of the island's major festivals. Local tourist offices will provide you with information on other events. If you happen to be in Alghero on the Saturday night before Carnival, head for the Via Carmine for the Festa della Cantina (Festival of the Wine Cellars). Throughout the night, the owners of cellars in the street offer wine and food to all and sundry, creating a lively party atmosphere.

Carnival mask

CALENDAR OF EVENTS

16 and 17 January Feast of Sant'Antonio Abate is celebrated in towns throughout the island, the festivities revolving around huge bonfires.

February Carnival is celebrated throughout the island during the week before Shrove Tuesday. Masks, costumes, loud music, song and dance are all part of the scene. Mamoiada's festival (which also takes place on 16 and 17 January) features the procession of the red-waist-coated *Issohadores* (the hunters) and the black-masked *Mamuthones* (the hunted). Oristano hosts the *Sa Sartiglia*, a medieval equestrian pageant (see page 49).

March–April Holy Week is marked by religious processions, Passion plays and street celebrations. Castelsardo is renowned for its Easter Monday *Lunissanti*, when a procession of white-hooded men winds its way through the town, to the accompaniment of chants. Oliena is famous for its Easter festivals, with processions on Good Friday and Easter Sunday. Other major events take place in Alghero, Sassari, Castelsardo and Ittireddu.

1–4 May In Cagliari's Festa di Sant'Efisio, an effigy of the saint is paraded from the Chiesa di Sant'Efisio as far as Pula and Nora, then back to the city.

Penultimate Sunday in May (Ascension Day) Sassari celebrates the *Cavalcata Sarda* with parades, dance, poetry and music, culminating in horse races, with knights in historical costume.

24 June San Giovanni Battista: the summer solstice is marked by festivities and bonfires in several towns and villages.

6–8 July The S'Ardia at Sedilo is Sardinia's equivalent to Siena's *Il Palio* – three days of daredevil horse racing.

14 August I *Candelieri*, held in thanksgiving to the Madonna for saving the Sassaresi from a plague in the 16th century, is named after the huge candles that are paraded through Sassari.

Penultimate or last Sunday of August Nuoro's major Festa del Redentore features colourful parades and folk dancing displays.

Last Sunday of October Aritzo, in the heart of the island, celebrates the *Sagra delle Castagne* or chestnut harvest.

25 December Processions take place in the lead up to Christmas (Natale), but the day itself is a low-key family event.

EATING OUT

Contrary to the assumption of many foreigners, the island's name has nothing to do with sardines. The surrounding waters are rich in fish, but Sardinia is not traditionally a seafaring island, and its culinary traditions are meat- rather than fish-based. Typical Sard cuisine is rustic and hearty: roast suckling pig and game, thick and filling soups, pasta with rich meat sauces. Eating out on the island rarely disappoints. The quality is good, the helpings generous (often huge) and the prices fair. Each region has its specialities, whether it's sun-dried mullet roe from Cabras, *zuppa quatta* (a bread and cheese soup) from Gallura or roasted snails from Sassari. Colonisers of the island left their culinary mark, as in the *paella* and other Catalan dishes of Alghero and the Ligurian and Tunisian flavours on the island of San Pietro. Fish naturally predominates along the coast, and menus offer a good range of seafood or simply grilled or baked whole fish. If you are lucky it will be the morning's catch; but as Mediterranean supplies dwindle, frozen fish – caught a long way from Sardinian shores – increasingly become the norm.

Tilicas and coricheddus (little hearts) are typical Sardinian biscuits

WHERE TO EAT

Traditionally, *ristoranti* or restaurants are smarter and more expensive than trattorias, but these days there is little difference between the two. Like the rest of Italy, Sardinia has a proliferation of pizzerias, which are less expensive than restaurants and popular with families. The best ones use wood-fired ovens *(forno a legna)* but apart from Sundays, these are only open in the evenings. Some pizzerias double up as trattorias, offering three-course meals as well as pizzas. In the towns you can often find places serving cheap slices of pizza *(al taglio)*. A *tavola calda* is a self-service or take-away, serving pasta, risottos, meat and vegetable dishes. The settings are unremarkable but costs are cut by the absence of service and cover charges. If all you want is a snack, stop at a bar or café. If you stand at the bar for *panini* (filled bread rolls) or *tramezzini* (crustless sandwiches, often with very generous fillings) instead of sitting on the terrace with waiter service, you will avoid service charges.

> ### When to eat
>
> Local people tend to eat lunch *(pranzo)* from around 12.30–1 to 3pm and dinner *(cena)* 8–10pm or later. Most restaurants close one day a week, and this is often Monday when the fish markets are closed. However, closing days are staggered so you can always find somewhere open.

WHAT TO EAT

In the Italian rather than Sardinian tradition, restaurant menus will offer a choice of *antipasti* (starters). This is likely to include a selection of cold meats such as local salamis, mountain hams and seasoned sausages, local sheep's cheeses and olives. Fish starters normally feature a seafood salad, dried mullet or tuna roe, or smoked fish. Some places serve an

antipasto misto (mixed starter) from a table, buffet-style, which can be a meal in itself.

Il primo is the first course, pasta or soup, which comes before *il secondo*, the meat or fish dish. Sardinian pasta comes in all shapes and sizes, is often home-made and is served with a wide range of sauces. Frequently found island specialities are *malloreddus* (also called *gnocchetti*), saffron-flavoured shell-shaped pasta, which is often served *alla campidanese* (with a spicy sausage and tomato sauce) and *culurgiones*, large ravioli stuffed with potato purée, egg, mint, garlic and cheese, served in a tomato or meat sauce. Another favourite is *fregula*, a couscous-like pasta served with clams or used in soups. Most menus offer a range of seafood pastas, typically *alla bottarga* (with mullet roe, garlic and olive oil), *ai ricci* (with sea urchins), *alle arselle* (with clams) or *all'aragosta* (with spiny lobster). *Zuppa di pesce* (fish soup) is usually excellent, but often has to be ordered in advance. *Sa Cassola* is a Spanish-influenced soup with fish, shellfish tomatoes and white wine; *zuppa di frutti di mare* or seafood soup is likely to include clams, mussels and prawns. In the south you will find the Ligurian-influenced *burrida*, made here with *gattucci di mare* or 'little sea cats', which are in fact dogfish, marinaded and cooked with parsley, garlic, ground walnuts and vinegar.

Main Courses

Sardinia's best known meat dish is *porchetto* (also called *porcetto* and *porceddu*) – suckling pig. Traditionally, a young pig is gently roasted on a spit, flavoured with myrtle, rosemary, laurel and sage, and served on cork trays with *pane carasau* and myrtle leaves. At best it's succulent and meaty, at worst tough and gristly. *Capretto* (kid goat) is done in the same way, though it's not quite as common. Goat is also used to make a rich casserole, cooked with artichokes and wine *(stufato di capretto)*. Typical

Hand-made *malloreddus*,
Sardinian gnocchi

main course meats are roast pork, chicken, wild boar and lamb, although the choice varies according to the season. A favourite is *agnello allo spiedo*, spit-roast lamb, best eaten in December. Vegetables come separately and are not a Sardinian strong point. Artichokes (sometimes served with peas), aubergines and asparagus are usually the best bets. Salads are invariably *verde* (green, that is, lettuce only) or *misto* (mixed, with tomato).

On the coast, fish fans are spoilt for choice. In many restaurants on or near the sea the menu is 80 percent fish-based. Seafood will include *anguille* (eels), *gamberi* (prawns), *calamari* (squid), *arselle* (clams) and, at the top end of the scale, *aragosta* (lobster), in season from March to the end of August. This is a speciality of Alghero, served Catalan-style, with tomatoes and onions, but it can be found in fish restaurants throughout the island. Cheaper options are *orata* (gilthead bream), *tonno* (tuna), *sogliola* (sole), *spigola* (seabass), *cefalo* (grey mullet) and *pesce spada* (swordfish). Fish is either grilled, lightly fried, baked or served in a marinade or white wine sauce. The smaller fish are served whole at a set price, the larger (for example, swordfish and tuna) will usually be charged by the *etto* (100g). It's quite normal to ask to see the size of a portion first, and check the price. A more acquired taste is *bottarga* or dried mullet roe ('peasants' caviar'), a speciality of Cabras in Oristano where the fish are caught. The eggs are salted, sun-dried between planks, cut into thin slices and served sliced as a starter with extra virgin olive oil or grated over pasta. The island of San Pietro

⊙ ENTRAILS AND ROTTEN CHEESE

Sardinian cuisine caters for many tastes and not all the local dishes will appeal to outsiders. Don't be surprised to find horse or donkey steak (*bistecche di cavallo* or *asinello*) on the menu, or restaurants where the older local customers are relishing the innards of calf, veal, lamb, goat or suckling pig. Visitors with adventurous tastes might like to try some of the traditional specialities from Sassari: *imino rosso*, red intestinal meats including heart and the diaphragm; the rarer *zimino bianco* (white entrails); *fidigheglia a s'ardares*, lambs' intestines with onions, garlic, parsley and white-wine vinegar; *sa cordula*, lambs' entrails roasted or barbecued on a spit; or *trippa alla parmigiana* (tripe with parmesan). Snails (*lumache* or *monzette*) also feature on menus.

One of the weirdest delicacies of the island is *casu beccio* or *casu marzu*, a strong, creamy cheese full of live maggots. You won't find it sold commercially and to sample it you will have to ask around and hunt down the farmers who make it. The saying goes that anything that doesn't kill you can feed you.

specialises in tuna, caught during the *mattanza* (see page 38) in May and early June. The infinite ways of dishing up the fish, whether fresh, smoked, marinated, served with oil and lemon or in thin, meat-like slices, will astonish anyone who is only familiar with tuna from the tin.

Bread and Cheese

The crisp, paper-thin *carasau* or *carta da musica*, served in restaurants all over the island, was traditionally made for shepherds when they were away for long periods. *Carasau* comes in various versions: *pane guttiau* is *carasau* dipped in olive oil and salted, served warm; *pane frattau* (also known as *pistoccu*) comes from the Barbagia area and is served with tomato sauce, pecorino cheese and eggs.

The island is well known for its cheeses, and most of Italy's *pecorino* is produced here. Made from ewes' milk it comes in various forms, most commonly the *pecorino romano* and the stronger *pecorino sardo* which is matured for three to 12 months. The sheep's milk from Barbagia is used to make *fiore sardo*, another pecorino, which is matured for several months. *Pecorino* is frequently used in Sardinian cuisine, as is the creamy *ricotta*, also made from ewes' milk.

Desserts

Sardinians don't excel at desserts despite the abundance of fruit produced on the island. The favourite way to end a meal is with pastries or cakes. Featuring on most menus are *seadas* (or *sebadas*), light pastries filled with ricotta and lemon zest, sprinked with sugar, deep fried and served with Sardinian honey; similar to *seadas* are *pardulas*, filled with ewes' cheese or ricotta, and flavoured with orange and saffron. Lighter options are fresh fruit or *gelati* (ice creams).

Alfresco drinks in Olbia

Wines

Formerly associated with sweet or fortified wines, Sardinia has made great headway in producing lighter wines to suit contemporary tastes. There are now around 20 wines of DOC status (*Denominazione di Origine Controllata*, indicating a quality wine), most of it coming from cooperatives. Vermentino dominates the dry whites, and notably the amber-coloured, slightly astringent Vermentino di Gallura produced in the hills in the north of the island. This is the only Sardinian wine classified as DOCG (Denominazione di Origine Controllata Garantita), identifying it as a wine from an established wine-producing region maintaining consistently high standards of quality. The best Vermentinos can be sampled at the hilltop wine museum in Berchidda, a wine-producing village of inland Gallusa. Another excellent white which goes well with fish is the dry Torbato, from Alghero; the sparkling version, Torbato Brut, makes a refreshing aperitif.

> **Wine and water**
>
> In restaurants, wine by the glass is almost unheard of, and half bottles can be hard to come by. Bottled water, either still or sparkling, is available in all restaurants, but you can always ask for tap water, which is perfectly safe to drink.

The best reds are the full-bodied dry Canonnaus, produced mainly around the Gennargentu massif but available throughout the island. The wine is a perfect accompaniment to red meat, game and cheese. The numerous variations of Canonnau include a strong rosé, which goes particularly well with roast suckling pig. Monica wine, a strong dry red produced in the Cagliari district, is similar in flavour to the best red Canonnau, but not as full-bodied. Worth trying too is Carignano del Sulcis, a smooth, full-bodied dry red.

House wine, *vino della casa*, is variable in quality but often perfectly drinkable and very reasonably priced. In the cheaper establishments it will be served in litre or half-litre carafes or jugs. At the other end of the scale, sophisticated restaurants will produce lengthy wine lists featuring international as well as Italian and Sardinian wines.

Harvesting grapes

Dessert Wines and Liqueurs

The most distinctive dessert wine of Sardinia is the Vernaccia di Oristano, produced from vines at the mouth of the River Tirso. Amber-coloured and with a hint of bitter almonds, the wine has an alcoholic content of about 15 degrees or more – it's certainly not to everyone's taste. You may well be offered a complimentary glass before or after a meal. Malvasia from Bosa and Cagliari is similar to Vernaccia and is often served with dessert. The drier sherry-like version is sometimes drunk by locals as a table wine, accompanying fish. Anghelu Ruju from Alghero, a strong, sweet red, makes a fine dessert wine. Another favourite is the sweet white Moscato, either still or sparkling, produced from the Muscat grape, which grows in the southwest of the island.

A good meal is usually concluded with a glass of liqueur or a choice of *amari* (bitters). At some stage of your stay you are bound to be offered a glass of *mirto*, the ubiquitous herbal liqueur distilled from myrtle, which grows all over the island. The superior reddish *mirto rosso* is distilled from the wild myrtle berries, the clear *mirto bianco* from myrtle leaves. The island's favourite firewater is the grappa-like *filu e ferru* (iron wire) made from grape skins. To conceal the evidence of illegal home distillation, farmers used to bury the bottles and use thin iron wires to mark the spot – hence the unusual name.

TO HELP YOU ORDER...

A table for one/two/three please **Un tavolo per una persona/per due/per tre, per favore**
I would like **Vorrei...**
What would you recommend? **Cosa ci consiglia?**
How much is it? **Quanto costa?**
The bill please **Il conto per favore**

As well as the regional specialities mentioned earlier, here are some words you are likely to see on Sardinian menus.

acqua water
aglio garlic
anguilla eel
basilica basil
birra beer
burro butter
carciofo artichoke
cinghiale wild boar
cipolle onions
coniglio rabbit
fagioli beans
fagiolini green beans
finnochio fennel
formaggio cheese
frittata omelette
frutti di mare seafood
funghi mushrooms
gamberetti shrimps
gamberi prawns
gelato ice cream
insalata salad
maiale pork

manzo beef
melanzane aubergine
monzette snails
olio oil
olive olives
ostriche oysters
pane bread
panna cream
patate potatoes
peperoni peppers
pesce fish
piselli peas
pollo chicken
polpo/pólipo octopus
pomodori tomatoes
prosciutto ham
riso rice
salsiccia sausage
spinaci spinage
uova eggs
vitello veal
zucchini courgettes

PLACES TO EAT

We have used the following symbols to give an idea of the price for a basic three-course evening meal for one, excluding wine:

€€€€ over 50 euros
€€€ 35–50 euros
€€ 25–35 euros
€ below 25 euros

ALGHERO AND THE NORTHWEST

Alghero

Al Tuguri €€€ *Via Maiorca 113, tel: 0799-76772, www.altuguri.it.* Alghero's most elegant restaurant, occupying two little rooms in an old mansion. Its reputation is based on fish, and the menu depends on the catch of the day. Typically it will include sea bass, sea bream, mullet and the full range of seafood, including lobster served in the Catalan or Aragonese style and sea urchins *(ricci del mare)* when in season (November to April). Closed Sunday.

Azienda Sa Mandra €€ *Strada Aeroporto Civile 21/a, tel: 0799-99150, www.aziendasamandra.it.* You should book in advance for this *agriturismo*, 3km (2 miles) from Alghero's airport. Hearty Sardinian fare based on traditional recipes from the Barbagia region, with meat cooked in a large outdoor fireplace. Accommodation is also available.

Caffè Latino € *Bastioni Magellano 10, tel: 0799-76541.* The attraction here is not so much the food as the setting on the Maddalena bastion, and the glorious sea views from the esplanade. Even off-season you may have to wait for a terrace table. No main meals, but snacks are available all day. It's the perfect spot for a pre-dinner aperitif.

La Lepanto €€€ *Via Carlo Alberto 135, tel: 0799-79116.* The sea-view setting and the tempting display of fresh fish make this one of Alghero's most sought-after restaurants. Lobster is served in a variety of ways, especially memorable with a mousse of ricotta, celery, parsley, basil and tomato.

Bosa

Borgo Sant'Ignazio €€–€€€ *Via Sant'Ignazio 33, tel: 0785-374 129,* www.ristorantebosa.it. Fresh fish and home-made pasta with seafood sauces are the favourites at this enticing restaurant in the old town. Specialities are the clam and mussel soup, the carpaccio of artichoke with smoked *bottarga* (mullet roe), black ravioli with cuttlefish and scampi sauce, and *panadas* (home-made pastries with beef, pork, mussels and artichokes).

Castelsardo

Il Cormorano €€€ *Via Colombo 5, tel: 0794-70628,* www.ristoranteilcormorano.net. On the edge of the historic centre and popular for fish and seafood, cheerful decor and professional service. Pastas come with mussels, spiny lobster, cockles and sea urchins, and can be followed by smoked tuna or fresh mullet, bream, sole or lobster. Choose from around 300 different wines or go with the excellent *vino da casa*. Closed Tuesday off-season.

Sassari

L'Assassino €–€€ *Via Pettenadu 19, tel: 0792-33463.* An atmospheric and typically Sardinian trattoria hidden away near pretty Piazza Tola in the old town. There are traditional and affordable pasta and meat dishes and, for visitors with adventurous tastes, local specialities such as pigs' trotters, donkey steaks, sweetbreads and *sa cordula* – sheep's entrails with peas. Closed Sunday.

Stintino

Silvestrino €€€ *Via Sassari 14, tel: 0795-23007,* www.hotelsilvestrino.it. At this fish restaurant in the Hotel Silvestrino, a homely dining room and

summer veranda are the setting for seafood risottos, lobster soup, *baci alla Silvestrino* (delicate pastries with spinach and ricotta) and *fregula sarda ai crostacei* (pasta with shellfish).

COSTA SMERALDA AND THE NORTHEAST

Calangianus

Il Tirabusciò €€ *Via Nino Bixio 5, tel: 0796-661849.* Rustic, cosy restaurant in the centre of town popular with the locals. Expect freshly made pastas and many other local dishes, such as *fregula* with gambas and mussels, with a wonderful selection of local wines.

Cannigione

La Colti €–€€ *Strada Arzachena–Cannigione, tel: 0789-88440.* An *agriturismo* in rural Gallura serving locally grown organic vegetables, homemade soups and pastas, suckling pig and wild boar, washed down with local wine, followed by *seadas* (cheese pastries with honey) and a glass of *mirto* (myrtle liqueur) on the house. Closed in winter.

Olbia

Bacchus €€€ *Via degli Astronauti 2, tel: 0789-651 010,* www.jazzhotel.it. Located in the Jazz Hotel, this modern, smart restaurant serves a vast selection of local and Mediterranean dishes prepared by chef Agostino Vinci. The food is good value for money and vegetarian and gluten-free options are available. The service is particularly attentive which combined with fine cuisine makes for a great dining experience.

Palau

Da Robertino €€–€€€ *Via Nazionale 20, tel: 0789-709 610.* Outstanding fish, whether it's marinated anchovies, *misto di mare* (fried seafood), mussels *alla marinara*, octopus salad, spaghetti *alle arselle* (with clams) or *bottarga* (mullet roe, salted and dried). Booking essential. Closed Mon and Jan–mid-Feb.

Santa Teresa di Gallura

Tropican €–€€€ *Spiaggia Rena Bianca, tel: 0391-138 6210.* The enticing setting right on the main beach, overlooking the Strait of Bonifacio, makes this a firm favourite with visitors. Choose from pizzas, pasta and simply grilled fish and meat. Wide choice of wines. Closed off-season.

NUORO AND THE EAST

Dorgali

Ristorante Ispinigoli €€ *Hotel Ispinigoli, Dorgoli, tel: 0784-95268, www. hotelispinigoli.it.* This capacious restaurant serves fish and spit roasts to tourists visiting the stunning Ispinigoli caves across the road. The panoramic dining area overlooks craggy hills, with the Gulf of Orosei visible in the far distance.

Nuoro

Canne al Vento €€ *Via Biasi 159, tel: 0784-201 762, www.ristorantecan nealvento-nuoro.it.* The menu concentrates on traditional Barbagia fare: prosciutto from Olieno, suckling pig, wild boar and horse meat, served with fresh local vegetables. A characteristic regional starter is *pane frattau* (crisp sheets of bread served with tomato sauce, eggs and pecorino cheese). Don't miss out on the delicious Sardinian desserts, and notably the *sebadas* (fried ricotta-filled pastries with honey). Closed Sunday.

Su Nugoresu € *Piazza San Giovanni 7, tel: 0784-258 017.* Simple and homely little trattoria/pizzeria on the central piazza, specialising in typical fish and meat dishes of the region.

Oliena

Su Gologone €€€€ *Località Su Gologone, Oliena, tel: 0784-287 512, www. sugologone.it.* In the wild Supramonte hill country, the Su Gologone has been renowned since 1960 for its country cuisine. It is also a hotel with 68 rooms, so reservations are essential. Suckling pig, goat and lamb are roasted on spits in the huge fireplace while guests tuck into smoked hams, salamis, cheeses and home-made pastas. For those with a hearty appetite, the taster menu is the best way to try all the specialities. The flower-decked terrace, overlooking the hills, is a lovely spot to dine. Closed off-season.

ORISTANO AND THE WEST

Cabras

Il Caminetto €€ *Via Battisti 8, tel: 0783-391 139, www.ristorante-ilcami* netto.com. Large, smart restaurant in the centre of Cabras serving mullet from the nearby lagoon. You can have it either simply grilled, salted and cooked in herbs, or flavouring spaghetti in its sundried roe form *(spaghetti alla bottarga)*. Closed Monday.

Oristano

Craf da Banana €€€ *Via de Castro 34, tel: 0783-70669, www.ristorante* crafdabanana.it. A convivial trattoria with brick vaults and old photographs of Oristano. This is a good place to try the island's specialities, whether it's Sardinian pasta dishes, gilthead bass cooked in the local Vernaccia wine, wild boar or – less likely to appeal to tourists but quite tender and tasty – *asino al vermentino e funghi* (donkey cooked with vermentino wine and mushrooms). Meals are usually rounded off with a small glass of Vernaccia. Closed Sunday.

Da Gino €€ *Via Tirso, 13, tel: 0783-71428.* This centrally located family-run trattoria is a good bet for local dishes such as *spaghetti ai ricci* (with sea urchins) and *tagliattelle con carciofi e bottarga* (with artichokes and mullet roe). Or push the boat out and opt for Gino's lobster. Closed Sunday.

CAGLIARI AND THE SOUTHEAST

Antica Hostaria €€€ *Via Cavour 60, tel: 0706-65870, www.anticahostaria.* it. A long-established restaurant with an elegant, intimate setting. Fresh flowers grace the tables and the pink walls are packed with paintings by the owner's brother. The chef's recommendations change every other day but you can expect to find delicious pastas with seafood or meat sauces, carefully prepared fresh fish dishes and some fine Sardinian wines.

Dal Corsaro €€€€ *Viale Regina Margherita 28, tel: 0706-64318*, www.stefanodeidda.it. Save this for a special occasion. It is among the finest restaurants on the island, with a Michelin star to its name, serving exquisite dishes in very formal, elegant surroundings, with prices to match. The specialities are mainly fish-based and include mussel and clam soup, monkfish, cuttlefish and sea snails.

Italia €€€ *Via Sardegna 26A, tel: 0706-57987.* One of the oldest restaurants in town, established (on the other side of the road) in 1921 and run by the Mundula family ever since. Customers are welcomed with an aperitif, then can choose between the 'bistro' downstairs or the slightly more elegant and expensive upstairs restaurant. Typical dishes here are seafood *antipasti*, fish soup, *fregula con arselle* (couscous-type pasta with clams) and spit-roast pork. Closed Sunday.

Lilliccu €€ *Via Sardegna 78, tel: 0706-52970*, www.trattoria.cagliari.it. Not one of the most conspicuous trattorias along Via Sardegna, with its dark exterior and net curtains, but emphasis here is on food rather than setting. It was established more than 80 years ago, and local people flock here for the professionally prepared fish dishes and Sardinian specialities at affordable prices. The fish soup is legendary; it is normally served on Tuesday and Friday and should be ordered in advance. Complimentary glasses of *mirto* usually follow the meal.

Villasimius

Stella d'Oro €€ *Via Vittorio Emanuele 25, tel: 0707-91255*, www.hotellastelladoro.com. One of the first restaurants in the region, founded in 1926. The German novelist Ernst Jünger was the first visitor to stay here when it became a hotel in the 1950s. It is a family-run, unpretentious place with a delightful courtyard and a central fountain for al fresco dining. Among the favourite dishes are *malfatti* (ricotta with spinach) and fish soup and lobster, which must be ordered in advance.

THE SOUTHWEST

Capoterra

Sa Cardiga e Su Schironi €€–€€€ *Località Maddalena Spiaggia, 10km (6 miles) southwest of Cagliari, tel: 0707-1652*, www.sacardigaesuschironi. it. Set in an unprepossessing area on the coast between Cagliari and Pula, this is one of the best seafood restaurants on the island. It's a huge place, usually full of local customers, and popular for weddings and parties. A wonderful array of fish and seafood are displayed in a boat inside the restaurant. Closed Monday except August.

Iglesias

Gazebo Medioevale €€ *Via Musio 21, tel: 0781-30871*, www.gazebome dioevale.it. An atmospheric restaurant in the old town of Iglesias with medieval brick arches and masks on the walls. Fish predominates and varies according to the market. The favourite dessert is a home-made *semi-freddo*. Closed Sunday.

Isola di San Pietro

L'Osteria Della Tonnara €€€ *Corso Battellieri 36, tel: 0781-855-734*, www.ristorantedaandrea.it. Unpretentious, charming seafood restaurant located on the Carloforte seafront. There are many local dishes on offer but it's a great place to taste the local tuna (freshly caught tuna is only available from May till end June); try *ventresca di tonno* (red tuna stake) or *lasagnetta di tonno con gocce di pesto* (tuna and pesto lasagna).

A-Z TRAVEL TIPS

A SUMMARY OF PRACTICAL INFORMATION

A

ACCOMMODATION

All hotels are categorised from one to five stars or, at the very top end of the scale, 5-star deluxe. Stars assigned denote facilities and are no indicator of charm or atmosphere. Tourist offices abroad (see page 131) will provide a list of accommodation.

In high season you need to book well in advance. The most crowded and expensive times are Easter and mid-June to early September. Prices on the Costa Smeralda are prohibitive but get cheaper the further inland you go. In winter many hotels close down; those that remain open offer dramatically cut rates – particularly top category hotels. Breakfast is normally included in the room rate. Hotels with their own restaurant often insist on half-board (or occasionally even full-board) during the season. Most hotels demand a supplement for a room with a view.

Hotels may require confirmation of a reservation, and a deposit of one night's stay, payable by credit card, is often requested. Failure to turn up or to inform the hotel in advance of cancellation usually incurs the loss of the deposit.

An appealing alternative is an *agriturismo*, traditionally a working farm, although the majority now are modern properties, rather than picturesque old farm buildings. They have sprouted all over Sardinia, many of them in remote locations well away from coastal resorts. The properties vary widely – as do the prices – and government controls are very limited. There is often the option of eating in, and some *agriturismi*, using home-grown produce, are renowned for their cuisine. Some are equipped with kitchens and rented out on a weekly basis. For details, try www.agriturismo.net, www.agriturismo.it, www.agriturismo.com, www.agriturismi.it, or www.agriturist.it. Except in August, you are unlikely to have problems finding rooms.

The last few years have seen a big rise in the number of B&Bs in private homes, varying from ancient palazzi to modern suburban houses. Prices are roughly equivalent to a two-star hotel but generally offer better value. Online listings available at www.sardegnabb.eu.

> I'd like a single/double room **Vorrei una camera singola/ matrimoniale or doppia**
> with bathroom **con bagno**
> What's the rate per night? **Quanto si paga per notte?**

AIRPORTS

Sardinia is served by three main airports: Elmas at Cagliari (www.sogaer. it), Olbia–Costa Smeralda at Olbia (www.geasar.com) and Fertilia at Alghero (www.algheroairport.com). All three handle flights within Italy, as well as charter and scheduled flights from London and other European cities. Cagliari's airport is 6km (4 miles) from the centre; trains run every 20 minutes between 5am and 9pm and the journey time is about 5–7 minutes. Olbia's airport, 5km (3 miles) from the centre, has a bus service every 20 minutes to the city centre taking 10 minutes, and a summer bus service to Arzachena, Palau and Sant Teresa di Gallura to the north. From Fertilia there are hourly buses to Alghero, 10km (6 miles) away, taking 20 minutes. Logudoro Tours bus service (tel: 0792-81728; www. logudorotours.it) links the airport with Cagliari, via Oristano, connecting with Ryanair flights. Bus services also operate from the airport to Sassari, Bosa, Santa Teresa di Gallura, Stintino and Nuoro.

B

BUDGETING FOR YOUR TRIP

Generally speaking, prices are average for Italy, but there are wide variations, depending where you stay and the time of year. In popular resorts such as Santa Teresa di Gallura, hotel prices in August are double those in spring or autumn. In general the best value tends to be inland, especially the *agriturismi*. In high season expect to pay €130–200 for a comfortable double with bath or €80–100 in a cheap town hotel. In *agriturismi* you pay from €50 to €90 per person for half board. For a good

evening meal in a restaurant expect to pay €30–45, for a light lunch €15–20, coffee or soft drink €1–2.50, beer in a bar €2.50–4 and spirits €2–4, but up to €10 in a smart café on the Costa Smeralda. Bear in mind that drinks at the bar are far cheaper than those served at a terrace table. Entry fees to museums and archaeological sites vary from €2 to €12; entrance is free for EU citizens under 18 and over 65.

C

CAMPING

Sardinia has numerous designated sites, mainly around the coast. Some are huge complexes complete with pools, restaurants, shops and sports facilities. Accommodation may be in caravans or bungalows as well as ready-erected tents. Details of campsites can be found at www.campeggi.com or at www.camping.it. Alternatively, local tourist offices can supply lists for their area. Campsites are normally open from Easter to October. Camping rough is forbidden.

CAR HIRE

Although much of the island can be covered by bus or train, services tend to be slow and infrequent, so to really explore the island you need to hire a car. Bookings made and paid for in advance are usually cheaper than hiring a car once you are in Sardinia. Be sure to read the terms and conditions carefully before you go – local suppliers have a habit of making you pay for extras you may not need.

Cars can be picked up at the main airports, where the major companies have their outlets. Drivers must present their own national driving licence or one that is internationally recognised. There is a small additional charge for an extra driver. Credit card imprints are taken as a deposit and are normally the only form of payment acceptable. 'Inclusive' prices do not normally include personal accident insurance, windscreens, tyres and wheels. Make sure you return the car with a full tank of fuel – there are hefty refuelling charges if you fail to do so. Car hire is quite expensive at €250–300 a week for a small car, and petrol prices are high.

> I would like to hire a car **Vorrei noleggiare una macchina**
> for one day **per un giorno**
> for one week **per una settimana**

CLIMATE

Sardinia's climate is typical of the Mediterranean, with long, hot summers, warm springs and autumns and mild winters. A good time to go is May when it's usually warm and sunny, beaches are uncrowded and the countryside is strewn with wild flowers. Autumn is pleasant and the water is still warm enough for swimming in late September or even October. The really hot months are July and August when temperatures soar to 30°C (86°F) or more, but sea breezes bring welcome relief. Less pleasant are the *maestrale* and *ponente* winds (from the northwest and west respectively). In winter average coastal temperatures are 10–14°C (50–57°F); the interior is far colder and snow sometimes covers the highest peaks. Rain falls mainly in winter and autumn, with a few sudden showers in spring. Below are the average temperatures for Cagliari:

	J	F	M	A	M	J	J	A	S	O	N	D
Max												
°F	57	59	63	66	73	81	86	86	81	73	66	61
°C	14	15	17	19	23	27	30	30	27	23	19	16
Min												
°F	47	51	48	51	57	64	70	70	66	59	51	48
°C	7	11	9	11	14	18	21	21	19	15	11	9

CLOTHING

Wearing miniskirts, skimpy shorts or shoulderless garments in churches is likely to cause offence. Wearing scanty clothing or swimwear may also offend, especially in inland towns. Only the very smartest restaurants and those in top hotels require jacket-and-tie formality. Casual clothes are quite acceptable in most trattorias.

CRIME AND SAFETY

The crime rate in Sardinia is low and visitors can stroll through the streets without any threat. There are, however, occasional instances of petty theft and it's wise to take simple precautions: always lock car doors and never leave valuables visible inside; leave important documents and valuables in the hotel safe; wear a money bag or, if carrying a shoulder bag, make sure it faces away from the street to deter motorcyclists who can snatch bags at high speed.

> I want to report a theft **Voglio denunciare un furto**
> My wallet/passport/ticket has been stolen **Mi hanno rubato il portafoglio/il passaporto/il biglietto**

D

DRIVING

Entering Italy. To bring your car into Italy, you will need an international driving licence or valid national one, car registration papers, a motor insurance certificate, a red warning triangle in case of breakdown, a national identity sticker for your car, a visibility vest (in case of breakdown).

Main highways linking cities are mostly dual carriageways and are fast and surprisingly empty. There are no motorways (hence no tolls). The SS131 (Carlo Felice highway) links Cagliari in the south with Sassari and

Porto Torres in the north, with a branch linking Abbastanta and Olbia, via Nuoro. In remote areas, such as the Gennargentu mountains, roads are not so good and signposting is random. Detours to beaches along dirt tracks can be long and tiring, especially (as in the Costa Smeralda) when they come to a halt at a villa complex with no public access to the beach. Many of the most scenic routes are tortuous coastal or mountain roads where you need to watch out for reckless drivers overtaking on blind bends.

patente driving licence
libretto di circolazione car registration papers
carta verde green card

Rules of the Road. Drive on the right, pass on the left. Speed limits are 50km/h (30mph) in towns and built-up areas, 90km/h (55mph) on other roads and 110km/h (70mph) on main highways. At roundabouts the traffic from the right has the right of way. Seat belts are compulsory in the front and back, and children should be properly restrained. The blood alcohol limit is 0.05 percent (stricter than the UK which is 0.08 percent) and zero for those who have had their licences for less than three years; random breath tests do occur. It is compulsory to keep dipped headlights switched on (day as well as night) – though many drivers ignore the regulation.

Are we on the right road for...? **Siamo sulla strada giusta per...?**

Breakdowns. In case of accident or breakdown call 113 (general emergencies – police) or the Automobile Club of Italy on 803-116, which has an efficient 24-hour service available to foreign visitors for a fee.

> I've had a breakdown. **Ho avuto un guasto.**
> There's been an accident. **C'è stato un incidente.**

Petrol. Many petrol stations close from 12.30–3.30pm, but there are plenty of '24-hour' stations with self-service dispensers accepting euro notes and credit cards. Main highways plenty of petrol stations, but in remote regions they are sparse. Most accept credit cards.

> Fill it up please. **Faccia il pieno per favore.**

Parking. Finding a parking space in cities and main towns can be a nightmare – even off-season. If you are lucky enough to find a space, you may need to purchase a special 'scratchcard', only available from tobacconists and bars. The card has to be displayed in the car, with details of the date and time of parking. Other street parking is controlled by meters or parking attendants.

> Where's the nearest car park? **Dov'è il parcheggio più vicino?**
> Can I park here? **Posso parcheggiare qui?**

E

ELECTRICITY

The electrical current is 220V, AC; sockets take two-pin, round-pronged plugs. Visitors from the UK will require an adaptor. Visitors from the US will need a transformer for 110V appliances.

EMBASSIES

Australia: Via Antonio Bosio 5, 00161 Rome, tel: 06-852 721, www.italy.embassy.gov.au.

Canada: Via Zara 30, 00198 Rome, tel: 06-85444 1, www.canada.it.

Ireland: Villa Spada, Via Giacomo Medici 1, 00153 Rome, tel: 06- 585 2381, www.ambasciata-irlanda.it.

New Zealand: Via Clitunno 44, 00198 Rome, tel: 06-853 7501, www.nzembassy.com.

UK: Via XX Settembre 80a, 00187 Rome, tel: 06-4220 0001, www.ukinitaly.fco.gov.uk.

US: Via Vittorio Veneto 121, 00187 Rome, tel: 06-46741, https://it.usembassy.gov

EMERGENCIES

General emergencies: 113
Police: 112
Fire: 115
Ambulance: 118

Help! **Aiuto!**
Stop thief! **Al ladro!**

GETTING THERE

By Air. An increasing number of low-cost airlines now fly direct to Sardinia from the UK and other European destinations. Ryanair (www.ryanair.com) has regular flights from Stansted to Alghero. EasyJet (www.easyjet.com) flies from Stansted to Cagliari and from Gatwick and Bristol to Olbia. Scheduled airlines have been forced to cut the costs of flights to compete with low-cost airlines. British Airways (www.ba.com)

flies direct to Cagliari from Gatwick and from Heathrow to Olbia.

There are no direct flights from long-haul destinations. Passengers from the US, Canada, New Zealand and Australia can fly to Rome or Milan and take one of the many connecting flights to Sardinia, but it's worth comparing the cost of a cheap flight to London, and then a charter or flight with a low-cost airline to Sardinia.

By Ferry. Sardinia is well connected to Italian mainland ports. Ferry services operate to the island from Civitavecchia, Naples, Livorno, and Genoa; also from Palermo and Trapani in Sicily. The main ferry companies operating services to the mainland are Tirrenia (www.tirrenia. it) and Moby (www.moby.it). The shortest route between mainland Italy and Sardinia is Civitavecchia to Olbia, which takes 4–7 hours depending on the type of ferry. Prices vary accordingly. Many services operate from Easter to October only and some of the faster services are restricted to high season only. Sardinia also has ferry links with France, connecting Marseille with Porto Torres in the north (14–17 hours) from April to October 2–3 times weekly, and a regular all-year service between Bonifacio in Corsica and the resort of Santa Teresa di Gallura. Porto Torres also has a ferry connection to Barcelona.

H

HEALTH AND MEDICAL CARE

All EU countries have reciprocal arrangements for medical services. UK residents should obtain a European Health Insurance Card (EHIC), available from post offices or online (www.ehic.org.uk). This only covers medical care, not emergency repatriation costs or additional expenses. Post-Brexit, UK residents will need to check new regulations before travelling. To cover all eventualities a travel insurance policy is advisable, and for non-EU residents, essential. For insurance claims, make sure you keep all receipts for medical treatment and any medicines prescribed. Vaccinations are not needed, but take sunscreen and mosquito repellent in the summer. Tap water is safe to drink, unless you see the sign *'Acqua non potabile'*. However, many visitors prefer to copy the locals and drink mineral water.

A pharmacy *(farmacia)* is identified by a green cross. All main towns offer a 24-hour pharmacy service, with a night-time and Sunday rota. After-hours locations are listed in local papers and posted on all pharmacy doors. Italian pharmacists are well trained to deal with minor ailments and although they do not stock quantities of foreign medicines they can usually supply the local equivalent. If you need a doctor *(medico)* ask at the pharmacy or at your hotel. For serious cases or emergencies, dial 118 for an ambulance or head for the *Pronto Soccorso* (Accident and Emergency) of the local hospital. This will also deal with emergency dental treatment.

> I need a doctor/a dentist. **Ho bisogno di un medico/dentista.**
> Where's the nearest (all-night) chemist? **Dov'è la farmacia (di turno) più vicina?**

L

LANGUAGE

Sardinia has two languages – standard Italian and *Sardo* or Sardinian. The island tongue reflects a host of different influences; the roots are in Latin, but the language was later modified by the various European powers who invaded the island, notably the Spanish. In Alghero, an old version of Catalan can still be heard; on the island of Sant'Antioco a Ligurian dialect is still spoken. Each region has its own dialect, and some Sards can only communicate with each other in Italian, particularly in inland Sardinia, while on the coasts there is more emphasis on Italian than on Sardinian dialects.

The vast majority of tourists here are Italian, and although you will

find English speakers in the main resorts and towns, elsewhere local people are only likely to speak a smattering of English, if that. Sardinians are appreciative of visitors who speak some Italian and (unlike Florentines and Venetians) don't have the infuriating habit of replying in broken English when you speak to them in Italian.

LGBTQ TRAVELLERS

Sardinia is conservative compared with the cosmopolitan cities of northern Italy. Although not necessarily averse to gay couples travelling together, locals do not always tolerate overt displays of affection. There are a few gay bars and clubs, notably in Cagliari and Sassari. To find general information and listings of gay venues within Italy, contact ArciGay, the national gay rights organisation, tel: 051-095 7241, www.arcigay.it. For gay events in Sardinia check out www.associazionearc.eu or www.movimentomosessualesardo.org.

M

MAPS

Sardinia is such a large island that even the best maps don't mark every road. The best road maps are the Touring Club Italiano at 1:200,000 and the Automobile Club d'Italia at 1:275,000. Maps are available at bookstores and kiosks, but the better ones are more readily available in specialist map or travel book shops abroad.

MEDIA

Newspapers. English and foreign newspapers are available, usually a day late, in the cities and main resorts during the season. The *International Herald Tribune* is available in the main centres Monday–Saturday. The two main island newspapers are Cagliari's *L'Unione Sarda* (www. unionesarda.it) and Sassari's *La Nuova Sardegna* (*La Nuova*; http://lan uovasardegna.gelocal.it).

Television. An increasing number of hotels provide satellite TV, but you won't necessarily get English-language channels. As regards Italian TV, there are the state-run RAI 1, 2 3, 4 and 5 plus numerous private channels pouring out tacky soaps, films and ads. State-run radio stations, RAI 1, 2 and 3, mainly broadcast news bulletins and music.

Have you any English-language newspapers? **Avete giornali in inglese?**

MONEY

The unit of currency in Italy is the euro (€) divided into 100 cents. Euro notes come in denominations of 500, 200, 100, 50, 20, 10 and 5; coins in denominations of 2 and 1; then 50, 20, 10, 5, 2 and 1 cents.

Exchange Facilities. Banks and post offices offer the best rates, followed by bureaux de change and hotels. Some bureaux de change offer commission-free facilities, but the rate of exchange is usually higher than in banks. Travellers' cheques can be exchanged (you need your passport), but attract a high commission and sometimes a transaction fee. Not all hotels or shops accept travellers' cheques.

Credit Cards and ATMs. Major credit cards are accepted in most hotels and restaurants, petrol stations and stores. Some smaller hotels, *agriturismi*, B&Bs and simple trattorias will only accept cash. ATM machines (or Bancomats) are found all over the island.

I want to change some pounds/dollars **Desidero cambiare delle sterline/dei dollari.**
Do you accept travellers' cheques? **Accetta i travellers' cheques?**
Can I pay with a credit card? **Posso pagare con la carta di credito?**

O

OPENING TIMES

Major museums, archaeological sites and caves are open all day every day. Others vary widely, but most close for lunch, from 12.30 or 1pm–3.30 or 4.30pm and for one day a week, normally Monday. Archaeological sites often remain open until an hour before sunset. Most churches are open daily from 7 or 8am–12 or 12.30pm, and from 4 or 5pm–7 or 8pm. In general banks open Monday to Friday 8.30am–1 or 1.30pm and some also open for an hour or so in the afternoon from 2.30 or 3pm–4 or 5pm. Some banks also open on Saturday morning. Shops are open Monday–Saturday 8 or 9am–1pm, and 4 or 5pm–7 or 8pm, though some supermarkets and main town stores are open all day. In summer, tourist shops in main resorts such as Alghero are open until 10pm.

P

POLICE

The *Polizia Urbana*, or city police, regulate traffic and enforce local laws, while the *Carabinieri* are the armed military police who handle public law and order. The *Politizia Stradale* patrol the highways and other roads. In an emergency the Carabinieri can be reached on 112 – or you can ring the general emergency number, 113.

Where's the nearest police station? **Dov'è il posto di polizia più vicino?**

POST OFFICES

Main branches are open Monday to Friday 8.30am–6.30 or 7.30pm, Saturday 8.30am–12.30 or 1pm, sub-post offices Monday to Friday 8.30am–2pm, Saturday 8.30am–noon. The postal service is slow, and for important

communications it is best to use the more expensive express system. Main post offices offer a poste restante service. Correspondence should be addressed to Fermo Posta, Ufficio Postale Principale, followed by the name of the town where you wish to pick it up. You will need some form of identification (preferably your passport) on collection. Stamps *(francobolli)* can be bought from tobacconists *(tabacchi)*, as well as from post offices.

> I'd like a stamp for this letter/postcard. **Desidero un francobollo per questa lettera/cartolina.**

PUBLIC HOLIDAYS

Most shops shut on national public holidays. As well as the main holidays listed below, some towns also take a public holiday to celebrate the local saint's day.

1 January New Year's Day
6 January Epiphany
March/April Easter Monday
25 April Liberation Day
1 May Labour Day
15 August Ferragosto; Assumption Day
1 November All Saints' Day
8 December Feast of the Immaculate Conception
25 December Christmas
26 December St Stephen's Day

TELEPHONES

Calls can be made from public telephones with a prepaid phone card *(scheda telefónica)*, available from *tabacchi* or newspaper stands. Remember to rip off the perforated corner before calling. Payphones have

instructions in English for international and other calls. Post offices and tobacconists sell international telephone cards (€5 and €10) with a pin number which can be used from public telephones, land lines and mobiles. Instructions are given in English on the card. When phoning abroad, dial 00 for the international code, followed by the city or area code and then the number (omitting any initial 0). Calls can also be made with a charge card bought from your telephone company prior to travel. This is useful for telephoning from hotels, which levy hefty surcharges on long-distance calls. The cheapest time to telephone from Italy is 10pm to 8am on weekdays and all day Sunday. Italian area codes have now all been incorporated into the numbers, so even if you are calling from the same town you are telephoning, the code needs to be included. **Mobile Phones.** If your mobile phone cannot receive or make calls in Italy (check with your mobile company before leaving) you can purchase a SIM 'pay as you go' card *(scheda pre-pagata)* in any mobile phone shop and have a new mobile number for the length of your stay. Local mobile network operators include Tre (www.tre.it), Vodafone (www.vodafone.it) and Wind (www.wind.it). EU travellers pay domestic prices for roaming calls, SMS and data.

Please give me ... **Per favore, mi dia...**
a phone card **una scheda telefonica**
5 euros/25 euros **cinque euro/venticinque euro**

TIME ZONES

Like the rest of Italy, Sardinia is one hour ahead of Greenwich Mean Time (GMT).

New York	**Sardinia**	Jo'burg	Sydney	Auckland
7am	**noon**	1pm	9pm	11pm

TIPPING

A 10–15 percent service charge is often included in restaurant bills, and although a tip will be appreciated, no extra is expected. For quick service in bars, leave a coin or two with your till receipt when ordering. Taxi drivers do not expect a tip but it is normal to round up the fare.

TOILETS

Public ones are hard to find, but you can always use toilets in cafés and bars. Buying a drink at the same time will be appreciated.

TOURIST INFORMATION

Within Sardinia you will find a tourist office (Azienda Autonoma di Soggiorno e Turismo, or AAST) in most towns and main resorts. The majority are helpful and can supply you with maps, pamphlets and details of accommodation and local attractions. However, some of the staff in the smaller offices have a very limited command of English. Centres with no official tourist office may have a *Pro Loco* in the town hall which serves a similar purpose but is open for limited hours in summer only. Failing that you can always try the local tour agencies, who organise excursions and car hire, and can provide general information. Most tourist offices are open Monday to Friday 9am–1pm and 4–7pm, Saturday 9am–1pm, though some of the minor offices keep shorter hours. The Alghero office is the best equipped on the island, and is open from Monday to Friday 9am–1pm and 3.30–6.30pm, Sat–Sun 9am–1pm (www.algheroturismo.eu).

To obtain information on Sardinia prior to travel, visit www.sardegnaturismo.it or contact the Italian National Tourist Office (enit) in your home country (www.enit.it).

Main Tourist Offices in Sardinia

Alghero: Piazza Porta Terra 9, tel: 0799-79054, www.alghero-turismo.it.

Cagliari: Via Roma 145, tel: 070-677 7397, www.cagliariturismo.it.
Carbonia/Iglesias: Via Mazzini 39, tel: 0393-800 592, www.visitsul cis.it.
Olbia: Via Dante 1, tel: 0789-52206, www.olbiaturismo.it.
Oristano: Piazza Eleonora 18, tel: 0783-368 3210, www.gooristano.com.

> Where's the tourist office? **Dov'è l'ufficio turistico?**

TRANSPORT

Bus. The bus network covers virtually the whole island, including some of the tiniest villages in the mountainous interior. The services are provided by a number of different companies and tend to be faster than those of trains. The fast services operate between the main towns: Cagliari, Oristano, Sassari, Nuoro and Olbia – for example, Cagliari to Sassari takes three hours non-stop, or four with stops en route. Certain services, particularly those to beaches or other tourist attractions, operate only in the summer months. The main bus company is the Azienda Regionale Sarda Trasporti (ARST; www.arst.sardegna.it). From June to September tourist passes are available on their buses for one, two, three or four weeks. The large towns have good bus systems and the service is cheap. Tickets can be bought in advance in bars, tobacconists or newspaper stands and then stamped once you board the bus or by using the DropTicket app on your mobile phone.

Trains. Services are provided both by the state-run Ferrovie dello Stato (www.trenitalia.com) and the regional public transport company ARST (www.arst.sardegna.it). Trains are inexpensive but tend to be slow and services infrequent. Trenitalia provides a service linking main towns – for example, Cagliari to Sassari (3–3.5 hrs), Cagliari to Olbia (3.5–4 hrs) and Sassari to Oristano (2.5 hrs); ARST provides some of the local services and also runs the delightful *Trenino Verde* (www.treninoverde.com). The narrow-gauge 'Little Green Train' chugs its way through some of the most remote and beautiful regions of the island. Provided you don't mind nearly five hours in uncomfortable vintage carriages, and returning (if needs be) the next day, try out the route from Mandas, 69km (43 miles) from Cagliari, all the way to the port of Arbatax on the east coast. The service was set up in 1888; today it runs during summer months only and is primarily for tourists. The service also covers the Nuoro–Bosa route and several lines in the Sassari region. One of the most popular routes is Sassari–Tempio Pausania–Palau, through oaks and granite masses to Tempio Pausania, then descending to the north coast with beautiful views over the Arcipelago della Maddalena.

Ferries. Regular car-ferry services connect Palau in the north of the island with the island of La Maddalena, and Portovesme in the southwest with the Isola di San Pietro.

When is the next ferry/bus/train to...? **Quando parte il prossimo traghetto/autobus/treno per...?**
Where can I buy a ticket? **Dove posso comparare un biglietto?**
One way/roundtrip **Andata/andata e ritorno**

TRAVELLERS WITH DISABILITIES

Sardinia is not an easy place to get around for travellers with limited mobility, and few of the museums and archaeological sites have wheelchair access. Accessible Italy (http://accessibleitaly.com) is a good online resource. In the UK you can obtain further information from Disability Rights UK (Plexal 14 East Bay Lane, Queen Elizabeth Olympic Park tel: 0203 687 0790; www.disabilityrightsuk.org) and in the US from SATH (tel: 212-447 7284; www.sath.org).

V

VISAS AND ENTRY REQUIREMENTS

For citizens of EU countries, a valid passport or identity card is all that is needed to enter Italy for stays of up to 90 days. Citizens of Australia, Canada, New Zealand and the US need a valid passport.

Visas *(permesso di soggiorno)*. For stays of more than 90 days a visa or residence permit is needed. Contact your country's Italian embassy.

Customs. Free exchange of non-duty-free goods for personal use is allowed between EU countries. Refer to your home country's regulating organisation for a current complete list of import restrictions.

Currency restrictions. Amounts exceeding €10,000 or equivalent in another currency must be declared when travelling outside the EU.

W

WEBSITES AND INTERNET ACCESS

The official tourist site is www.sardegnaturismo.it. Also try:
www.sardiniapoint.it practical and cultural information.
www.ciaosardinia.com itineraries and public transport.
Internet cafés and points can be found in the main towns and resorts. You will need to present a passport or driving licence before using a public internet point.

Y

YOUTH HOSTELS

The island has seven official youth hostels including ones at Cagliari, Castelsardo and Alghero. For information and reservations (essential in summer), log on to www.aighostels.it (the Italian Youth Hostel Association) or www.hihostels.com (Hostelling International).

RECOMMENDED HOTELS

Tourism on the island didn't really take off until the 1960s and the typical Sardinian hotel is a modern, sea-view building, strong on facilities but short on charm and character. Those listed below stand out, either for setting, ambience, food, good value – or if you are lucky, all four. At the top end of the market are the exclusive hotels of the Costa Smeralda, which fetch some of the highest prices in Italy, and those of Santa Margherita di Pula, south of Cagliari. At the other end of the scale are the increasingly popular B&Bs (Bed and Breakfasts) and the now abundant *agriturismi* (see page 116), where you can stay on a farm or rural property and see the local way of life.

The symbols below are a rough indication of what you can expect to pay for a twin room with bathroom, including breakfast, in high season. Many hotels insist on half-board, especially in summer.

€€€€   over 250 euros
€€€   160–250 euros
€€   110–160 euros
€   below 110 euros

ALGHERO AND THE NORTHWEST

Alghero

Porto Conte €€€ *Località Porto Conte, tel: 0799-42035,* www.hotelpor toconte.com. Large but low-rise, Catalan-style hotel amid pines and palms right on the bay of Porto Conte. The pool and garden area lead on to a sandy beach, equipped with facilities (at extra cost) and beach club. Guest rooms look out on to the gardens or, ideally, across the clear blue waters of the bay.

San Francesco € *Via Ambrogio Machin 2, tel: 0799-80330,* www.sanfran cescohotel.com. A rather special place in that it's the only hotel in the old town, and the rooms focus on the lovely cloister of the church of San

Francesco. (The building used to be the convent for the church.) The only public area apart from reception is a basic breakfast room/bar off the cloister. The 20 bedrooms are nothing special, but they are clean and come with private bathrooms.

Villa Las Tronas €€€€ *Lungomare Valencia 1, tel: 0799-81818*, www.hotelvillalastronas.com. You can't miss this castellated building set on a private rocky promontory just south of Alghero. Built at the end of the 19th century, in the 1940s it was the holiday home of the Italian royal family. For many years it has been a small, exclusive and elegant hotel. Guest rooms have sea views, Art Nouveau furnishings and modern bathrooms. There is no beach, but you can swim in the indoor or outdoor seawater pools or from the rocky terraces around it. Facilities include a luxury spa with a beauty and fitness section.

Bosa

Corte Fiorita €–€€ *Via Lungo Temo de Gasperi, tel: 0785-377 058*, www.albergo-diffuso.it. Three of central Bosa's medieval buildings have been beautifully restored to form this rustic-style hotel. The main building (Le Palme), complete with breakfast room, patio and reading room, is a narrow four-storey house overlooking the River Temo; the annexe (I Gerani) is on a narrow alley nearby. All rooms have large bathrooms and some have balconies.

Sa Pischedda €–€€ *Via Roma 8, tel: 0785-373 065*, www.hotelsapischedda.com. Built in 1895 this was one of the first three hotels on the island. It has frescoes in reception and marble-topped antiques in public areas. Bedrooms are modern, smallish and sparsely furnished, some with capacity for four guests. The restaurant is well worth trying for lobster, fish soup or prawns, cooked in Malvasia wine.

Stintino

Silvestrino €€ *Via Sassari, 14, tel: 0795-23007*, www.hotelsilvestrino.it. A small, family-run hotel with a first-rate fish restaurant (see page 109), spotless guest rooms and a welcoming atmosphere. Located in

the centre of the fishing village, it has 11 rooms varying in size, comfort and price (the most desirable room is No. 25 at the top with its own solarium). Prices virtually double in summer – the village and the nearby Pelosa beach are hugely popular with tourists in season.

COSTA SMERALDA AND THE NORTHEAST

Arzachena

Ca' La Somara €–€€ *Arzachena, tel: 0789-98969*, www.calasomara.it. Only 4km (2.5 miles) from the Costa Smeralda, yet it couldn't be more different from the luxury hotels along the coast. A peaceful *agriturismo*, it was converted from sheep stables to provide a welcoming, relaxing and rural retreat. Donkeys graze nearby and the farmhouse retains its rustic features. Meals, using vegetables from the farm, are served on request. Walking and riding excursions can be arranged.

Cala di Volpe €€€€ *Porto Cervo, Costa Smeralda, tel: 0789-976 111*, www. caladivolpe.com. Exclusive and outrageously expensive, it was one of the first tourist hotels on the island, built in rustic style with arches, beams and rough-plastered walls. Facilities include a fabulous seawater pool, tennis, water sports, putting green, wellness centre and a private launch to the pristine white-sand beach.

Capriccioli €€€ *Porto Cervo, Costa Smeralda, tel: 0789-96004*, www.ho telcapriccioli.it. One of the less exorbitant hotels on this coast, it started life as a tiny family-run restaurant – the first on the Costa Smeralda. Now it's a 45-bedroom four-star hotel with a large sea-view restaurant, pool and tennis court. Bedrooms can be a bit cramped but are well equipped. Half-board is compulsory. Steps lead down to a pretty – and very popular – little beach.

Lu Pastruccialeddu € *Arzachena, tel: 0789-81777*, www.pastruccialeddu. com. This stone B&B with swimming pool has a peaceful setting with 50 hectares (124 acres) of private land, but is only 5km (3 miles) from the lovely beaches of the Costa Smeralda. The seven guest rooms have TV and private bathrooms. Breakfasts of delicious home-made pastries

and jams are served in a rustic dining room. Minimum stay four nights from mid-June to mid-September.

Santa Teresa di Gallura

Corallaro €€€ *Località Rena Bianca, 07028 Santa Teresa di Gallura, tel: 0789-755 475*, www.hotelcorallaro.it. Santa Teresa's best-known hotel, set back from the Rena Bianca beach in the centre. Surprisingly few rooms have sea views (you pay a hefty daily supplement for the privilege) but it's pleasantly light and airy throughout. Facilities include spacious public rooms, small gym, outdoor pool, restaurant and solarium.

La Funtana €€€ *Via Nazionale 69, 07028 Santa Teresa di Gallura, tel: 0789-741 025.* This relaxing Mediterranean-style hotel is surrounded by verdant gardens, while located near the Santa Teresa di Gallura's marina and within walking distance of the lively city centre. The hotel comprises of several buildings centred around the spacious courtyard and large swimming pool. The 53 rooms are comfortable and decorated in Sardinian style. The on-site restaurant serves gourmet fare.

NUORO AND THE EAST

Dorgali

L'Oasi € *Via García Lorca 13, 08022 Cala Gonone, tel: 0784-93111,* www.loasihotel.it. Family-run hotel occupying a wonderful spot high above the port, with sweeping views of the sea and coast. The buildings are set among gardens and pines, with terraces and balconies making the most of the views. A short cut takes you down to the port where there is a wide choice of boat excursions along the coast. Stays are normally for a minimum of three days, or seven days in August.

Oliena

Su Gologone €€€–€€€€ *Località Su Gologone, tel: 0784-287 512,* www.sugologone.it. Inland Sardinia's most famous hotel and restaurant, beautifully located among olive trees and pine woods below the Supramonte mountains. The restaurant (see page 111) is renowned for suckling pig, which sizzles in the huge fireplace in the dining room. Guest rooms are all prettily furnished with hand-embroidered local fabrics, and walls throughout are hung with artworks by island artists. Facilities include a large swimming pool, fitness centre, tennis courts and mini golf. Land-rover safaris into the Barbagia, horse riding and trekking are regularly organised.

ORISTANO AND THE WEST

Oristano

Eleonora € *Piazza Eleonora 12, tel: 0783-70435,* www.eleonora-bed-and-breakfast.com. This delightful B&B occupies two floors of an old *palazzo* overlooking the handsome 19th-century Piazza Eleonora in the heart of the old town. The large rooms retain original features and some antiques. Breakfasts are served in the garden in summer. No credit cards.

Piscinas

Le Dune €€€–€€€€ *Località Piscinas, Via Bau 1, Ingurtosu, 09031 Arbus, tel: 0709-77130,* http://ledunepiscinas.com. Stylish conversion of an old mining building on the glorious beach of Piscinas, accessed along a 7km (4.5-mile) dirt track from Ingurtosu. The 25 guest rooms have bamboo and rattan furnishings, and no televisions. Half- or full-board is compulsory. Facilities include a wellness and beauty centre and two restaurants, one on the beach.

Santu Lussurgiu

Antica Dimora del Gruccione € *Via Michele Obino 31, Santu Lussurgiu (35km/22 miles north of Oristano), tel: 0783-552 035,* www.anticadimora.com. This charming 17th-century mansion is an *albergo diffuso*, that is, a main house with other rooms dotted around the neighbourhood. As well as singles, doubles and triple rooms, there are suites with an open fireplace and kitchen. Cuisine in the restaurant is based on the Slow Food concept, using top quality local products. This is a good base for active

holidays, whether it's trekking, riding, diving, guided archaeological or nature tours, or boat trips.

CAGLIARI AND THE SOUTHEAST

Cagliari

BJ Vittoria Hotel € *Via Roma 75, tel: 0706-67970*, www.hotelbjvittoria.it. Friendly, family-run hotel on the third floor of a 1920s building overlooking the ferry port. Original features such as stucco ceilings have been preserved and bedrooms have good, solid furniture. Breakfast (which is extra) is served only in summer, but there are plenty of inviting cafés under the arcades of Via Roma.

T Hotel €€€ *Via dei Giudicati 66, tel: 0704-7400*, www.thotel.it. Cagliari's first designer hotel opened in 2005. Modern and stylish, it incorporates a 15-storey steel-and-glass round tower, whose upper floors have panoramic views. Guest rooms come with king-size beds and Ikea-style furnishing, along with vibrant shades of orange or red – or the more tranquil green or blue. Amenities include a minimalist bar and garden-view bistro, which are popular rendezvous for the Cagliaresi, and a wellness centre. Although more geared to business travellers than tourists (the hotel is about 2km/1 mile from the historic centre with few restaurants nearby), you can get rooms at bargain prices in summer when business trade declines.

Santa Margherita di Pula

Forte Village Resort €€€€ *09010 Santa Margherita di Pula, tel: 0709-218 818*, www.fortevillageresort.com. Vast luxury complex set in 22 hectares (55 acres) of gardens by the beach. The resort comprises eight hotels, all five- and four-star, 10 swimming pools, 21 restaurants, wellness centre, spa and numerous water sports. Excellent children's facilities include a mini-club, crèche and babysitting.

MarePineta €€€ *09010 Santa Margherita di Pula, tel: 0709-209 406*, www. hotelmarepineta.it. The cheaper sister of the nearby Hotel Flamingo, inconspicuously located among the beach-side pines. Accommodation is in attractively furnished individual bungalows behind the hotel, while public rooms focus on the sea and the white sandy beach. Guests have the use of the Flamingo facilities including spa and mini-club for children. Half-board only.

San Vito

Casa Camboni € *Via Nazionale 187, 09040 San Vito, tel: 328-0222 762,* www.casacamboni-guesthouse.com. There is no reason to visit the town of San Vito other than to stay at this splendid town mansion. The oldest part dates from 1800 and the house has been in the same family for four generations. From the main street a huge wooden portal opens on to a delightful courtyard where breakfasts are taken at a communal table. Guest rooms with wood floors and pine furnishings and good bathrooms have been converted at the back of the house.

Villasimius

Cala Caterina €€€€ *Via Lago Maggiore 32, Villasimius, tel: 070-798 029,* www.hotelcalacaterina.it. A peaceful and stylish retreat, this Mediterranean villa has lush gardens leading down to an enticing sandy cove. Guest rooms are decorated in pastel shades, with painted wooden furniture and colourful batik artwork. The bar terrace overlooks the pool and gardens, and the bay is equipped with sunbeds and parasols. If all this is not relaxing enough, there is always the beauty centre for a massage.

THE SOUTHWEST

Isola di San Pietro

Hieracon €€ *Corso Cavour 62, Carloforte, tel: 0781-854 028,* www. hotelhieracon.com. Art Nouveau hotel with an elegant pale facade, overlooking the port. Guest rooms in the main building, apartments in the garden, all with television and air conditioning. Breakfast in summer is taken in the shade of palm trees, other meals in the main restaurant with sea-view terrace tables.

DICTIONARY

adj adjective **adv** adverb **BE** British English **n** noun **prep** preposition **v** verb

A

a.m. del mattino
abbey l'abbazia
accept v accettare
access l'accesso
accident l'incidente
accommodation l'alloggio
account il conto
acupuncture l'agopuntura
adapter l'adattatore
address l'indirizzo
admission l'ingresso
after dopo; **~noon** il pomeriggio; **~shave** il dopobarba
age l'età
agency l'agenzia
AIDS l'AIDS
air l'aria; **~ condition-ing** l'aria condizio-nata; **~ pump** la pompa dell'aria; **~line** la compagnia aerea; **~mail** la posta aerea; **~plane** l'aereo; **~port** l'aeroporto
aisle il corridoio; **~ seat** il posto sul corridoio
allergic allergico; **~ reaction** la reazione allergica

allow v permettere
alone solo
alter v modificare
alternate route il percorso alternativo
aluminum foil la carta stagnola
amazing straordinario
ambulance l'ambulanza
American americano
amusement park il lunapark
and and
anemic anemico
anesthesia l'anestesia
animal l'animale
ankle la caviglia
antibiotic l'antibiotico
antiques store il negozio d'antiquariato
antiseptic cream la crema antisettica
anything qualsiasi cosa
apartment l'appartamento
appendix (body part) l'appendice
appetizer l'antipasto
appointment l'appuntamento
arcade la sala giochi

area code il prefisso
arm il braccio
aromatherapy l'aromaterapia
around (the corner) dietro di
arrivals (airport) gli arrivi
arrive v arrivare
artery l'arteria
arthritis l'artrite
art l'arte
aspirin l'aspirina
asthmatic asmatico
ATM il bancomat
attack l'aggressione
attend v frequentare
attraction (place) l'attrattiva
attractive attraente
Australia Australia
Australian australiano
automatic automatico; **~ car** l'auto col cambio automatico
available libero

B

baby il bebè; **~ bottle** il biberon; **~ wipe** la salvietta per neonati; **~sitter** la babysitter
back (body part) la

schiena; **~ache** il mal di schiena; **~pack** lo zaino
bag la borsa
baggage il bagaglio; **~ claim** il ritiro bagagli; **~ ticket** lo scontrino bagagli
bakery la panetteria
ballet lo spettacolo di danza
bandage la benda
bank la banca
bar il bar
barbecue il barbecue
barber il barbiere
baseball il baseball
basket (grocery store) il cestino
basketball il basketball
bathroom il bagno
battery la batteria
battleground il campo di battaglia
be v essere
beach la spiaggia
beautiful bello
bed il letto; **~ and breakfast** la pensione
begin v iniziare
before prima

beginner il principiante
behind dietro
beige beige
belt la cintura
berth la cuccetta
best il migliore
better migliore
bicycle la bicicletta
big grande
bigger più grande
bike route il percorso ciclabile
bikini il bikini; **~ wax** la ceretta all'inguine
bill *v* **(charge)** fatturare; **~** *n* **(money)** la banconota; **~** *n* **(of sale)** il conto
bird l'uccello
birthday il compleanno
black nero
bladder la vescica
bland insipido
blanket la coperta
bleed *v* sanguinare
blood il sangue; **~ pressure** la pressione sanguigna
blouse la camicetta
blue blu
board *v* imbarcarsi
boarding pass la carta d'imbarco
boat la barca
bone l'osso
book il libro; **~store** la libreria
boots gli stivali
boring noioso
botanical garden il giardino botanico

bother *v* infastidire
bottle la bottiglia; **~ opener** l'apribottiglie
bowl la coppa
box la scatola
boxing match l'incontro di boxe
boy il ragazzo; **~friend** il ragazzo
bra il reggiseno
bracelet il braccialetto
brakes (car) i freni
break *v* rompere; **~-in (burglary)** il furto con scasso; **~down** il guasto
breakfast la colazione
breast il petto; **~feed** *v* allattare
breathe *v* respirare
bridge il ponte
briefs (clothing) lo slip
bring *v* portare
British britannico(a)
broken rotto
brooch la spilla
broom la scopa
brother il fratello
brown marrone
bug l'insetto
building l'edificio
burn *v* bruciare
bus l'autobus; **~ station** la stazione degli autobus; **~ stop** la fermata del bus; **~ ticket** il biglietto del bus; **~ tour** l'escursione in pullman

business il lavoro; **~ card** il biglietto da visita; **~ center** il centro business; **~ class** la classe business; **~ hours** l'orario d'apertura
butcher il macellaio
buttocks le natiche
buy *v* comprare
bye ciao

C

cabaret il cabaret
cabin la cabina
cable car la funivia
cafe il caffè
call *v* chiamare; **~** *n* la chiamata
calories le calorie
camera la macchina fotografica; **digital ~** la macchina fotografica digitale; **~ case** l'astuccio della macchina fotografica; **~ store** il negozio di fotografia
camp *v* campeggiare; **~ stove** il fornello da campeggio; **~site** il campeggio
can opener l'apriscatole
Canada il Canada
Canadian canadese
cancel *v* annullare
candy le caramelle
canned good lo scatolame
canyon il canalone
car l'auto; **~ hire**

[BE] l'autonoleggio; **~ park [BE]** il parcheggio; **~ rental** l'autonoleggio; **~ seat** il seggiolino per auto
carafe la caraffa
card la carta; **ATM ~** il bancomat; **credit ~** la carta di credito; **debit ~** il bancomat; **phone ~** la scheda telefonica
carry on board *v* **[BE]** portare a bordo
carry-on il bagaglio a mano
cart (grocery store) il carrello; **~ (luggage)** il carrello
carton il cartone; **~ of cigarettes** la stecca di sigarette
case (container) la cassa
cash *v* incassare; **~** *n* i contanti; **~ advance** l'acconto
cashier il cassiere
casino il casinò
castle il castello
cathedral la cattedrale
cave la grotta
CD il CD
cell phone il telefonino
Celsius Celsius
centimeter il centimetro
certificate il certificato

chair la sedia; **~ lift** la seggiovia
change v **(buses)** cambiare; **~** v **(money)** cambiare; **~** v **(baby)** cambiare; **~** n **(money)** il cambio
charcoal il carbone
charge v **(credit card)** addebitare; **~** n **(cost)** il costo
cheap economico; **~er** più economico
check v **(on something)** controllare; **~** v **(luggage)** controllare; **~** n **(payment)** l'assegno; **~-in (hotel/airport)** il check-in; **~ing account** il conto corrente; **~-out (hotel)** il pagamento del conto
Cheers! Salute!
chemical toilet il WC da campeggio
chemist [BE] la farmacia
cheque [BE] l'assegno
chest (body part) il petto; **~ pain** il dolore al petto
chewing gum la gomma da masticare
child il bambino; **~ seat** il seggiolone; **~'s menu** il menù per bambino; **~'s portion** la porzione per bambino

Chinese cinese
chopsticks i bastoncini cinesi
church la chiesa
cigar il sigaro
cigarette la sigaretta
class la classe; **business ~** la classe business; **economy ~** la classe economica; **first ~** la prima classe
classical music la musica classica
clean v pulire; **~** adj pulito; **~ing product** il prodotto per la pulizia; **~ing supplies** i prodotti per la pulizia
clear v **(on an ATM)** cancellare
cliff la scogliera
cling film [BE] la pellicola per alimenti
close v **(a shop)** chiudere
close vicino
closed chiuso
clothing l'abbigliamento; **~ store** il negozio d'abbigliamento
club il club
coat il cappotto
coffee shop il caffè
coin la moneta
colander la scolapasta
cold (sickness) il raffreddore; **~ (temperature)** freddo

colleague il collega
cologne la colonia
color il colore
comb il pettine
come v venire
complaint il reclamo
computer il computer
concert il concerto; **~ hall** la sala da concerti
condition (medical) la condizione
conditioner il balsamo
condom il preservativo
conference la conferenza
confirm v confermare
congestion la congestione
connect v **(internet)** collegarsi
connection (internet) il collegamento; **~ (flight)** la coincidenza
constipated costipato
consulate il consolato
consultant il consulente
contact v contattare; **~ lens** la lente a contatto; **~ lens solution** la soluzione per lenti a contatto
contagious contagioso
convention hall la sala congressi
conveyor belt il nastro trasportatore
cook v cucinare
cooking gas il gas per cucina

cool (temperature) fresco
copper il rame
corkscrew il cavatappi
cost v costare
cot il lettino
cotton il cotone
cough v tossire; **~** n la tosse
country code il prefisso del paese
cover charge il coperto
crash v **(car)** fare un incidente
cream (ointment) la crema
credit card la carta di credito
crew neck a girocollo
crib la culla
crystal il cristallo
cup la tazza
currency la valuta; **~ exchange** il cambio valuta; **~ exchange office** l'ufficio di cambio
current account [BE] il conto corrente
customs la dogana
cut v **(hair)** tagliare; **~** n **(injury)** il taglio
cute carino
cycling il ciclismo

D

damage v danneggiare; **~d** danneggiato
dance v ballare; **~ club** il club di ballo; **~ing** il ballo

dangerous pericoloso
dark scuro
date (calendar) la data
day il giorno
deaf sordo
debit card il bancomat
deck chair la sedia a sdraio
declare v dichiarare
decline v **(credit card)** rifiutare
deeply profondamente
degrees (temperature) i gradi
delay v ritardare
delete v **(computer)** eliminare
delicatessen la gastronomia
delicious squisito
denim i jeans
dentist il dentista
denture la dentiera
deodorant il deodorante
department store il grande magazzino
departures (airport) le partenze
deposit v depositare; **~ (bank)** n il deposito; **~ (to reserve a room)** il deposito
desert il deserto
detergent il detersivo
develop v **(film)** sviluppare
diabetic diabetico
dial v comporre il numero
diamond il diamante

diaper il pannolino
diarrhea la diarrea
diesel il diesel
difficult difficile
digital digitale; **~ camera** la macchina fotografica digitale; **~ photos** le foto digitali; **~ prints** le stampe digitali
dining room la sala da pranzo
dinner la cena
direction la direzione
dirty sporco
disabled il disabile; **~ accessible [BE]** accessibile ai disabili
disconnect v **(computer)** scollegare
discount lo sconto
dish (kitchen) il piatto; **~washer** la lavastoviglie; **~washing liquid** il detersivo per i piatti
display lo schermo; **~ case** la vetrinetta
disposable usa e getta; **~ razor** la lametta usa e getta
dive v tuffarsi; **~ing equipment** l'attrezzatura subacquea
divorce v divorziare
dizzy stordito

doctor il medico
doll la bambola
dollar (U.S.) il dollaro
domestic domestico; **~ flight** il volo nazionale
door la porta
dormitory il dormitorio
double bed il letto matrimoniale
downtown (direction) il centro; **~ area** il centro
dozen la dozzina
drag lift lo ski lift
dress (piece of clothing) il vestito; **~ code** il codice di abbigliamento
drink v bere; **~** n la bevanda; **~ menu** il menù delle bevande; **~ing water** l'acqua potabile
drive v guidare
driver's license number il numero di patente
drop (medicine) la goccia
drowsiness la sonnolenza
dry cleaner il lavasecco
dubbed doppiato
during durante
duty (tax) la tassa; **~ free** duty free
DVD il DVD

E

ear l'orecchio; **~ache** il mal d'orecchio
earlier prima
early presto
earrings gli orecchini
east est
easy facile
eat v mangiare
economy class la classe economica
elbow il gomito
electric outlet la presa elettrica
elevator l'ascensore
e-mail v inviare e-mail; **~** n l'e-mail; **~ address** l'indirizzo e-mail
emergency l'emergenza; **~ exit** l'uscita d'emergenza
empty v svuotare
enamel (jewelry) lo smalto
end v finire
English inglese
engrave v incidere
enjoy v godersi
enter v entrare
entertainment l'intrattenimento
entrance l'entrata
envelope la busta
equipment l'attrezzatura
escalators le scale mobili
estate car [BE] la station wagon

e-ticket il biglietto elettronico
EU resident il residente UE
euro l'euro
evening la sera
excess l'eccesso
exchange v (money) cambiare; ~ *n* **(place)** il cambio; ~ **rate** il tasso di cambio
excursion l'escursione
excuse *v* scusare
exhausted esausto
exit *v* uscire; ~ *n* l'uscita
expensive caro
expert esperto
exposure (film) la posa
express espresso; ~ **bus** il bus espresso; ~ **train** il treno espresso
extension (phone) l'interno
extra extra; ~ **large** extra large
extract *v* **(tooth)** estrarre
eye l'occhio
eyebrow wax la ceretta per sopracciglie

F

face il viso
facial la pulizia del viso
family la famiglia
fan (appliance) il ventilatore; ~ **(sou-**
venir) il ventaglio
far lontano; **~-sighted** ipermetrope
farm la fattoria
fast veloce; ~ **food** il fast food
faster più veloce
fat free senza grassi
father il padre
fax *v* inviare per fax; ~ *n* il fax; ~ **number** il numero di fax
fee la tariffa
feed *v* dare da mangiare
ferry il traghetto
fever la febbre
field (sports) il campo
fill *v* riempire; ~ **out** *v* **(form)** compilare; **~ing (tooth)** l'otturazione
film (camera) il rullino
fine (fee for breaking law) la multa
finger il dito; **~nail** l'unghia
fire il fuoco; ~ **department** i vigili del fuoco; ~ **door** la porta antincendio
first primo; ~ **class** la prima classe
fit (clothing) *v* andare bene
fitting room il camerino
fix *v* **(repair)** riparare
flashlight la torcia elettrica
flat tire la gomma
a terra
flight il volo
floor il pavimento
flower il fiore
folk music la musica folk
food il cibo
foot il piede
football game [BE] la partita di football
for per
forecast la previsione
forest il bosco
fork la forchetta
form il modulo
formula (baby) il latte in polvere
fort la fortezza
fountain la fontana
free libero
freezer il freezer
fresh fresco
friend l'amico
frying pan la padella
full-service il servizio completo
full-time a tempo pieno

G

game la partita
garage il garage
garbage bag il sacchetto per la spazzatura
gas (cooking) il gas per cucina; ~ **(heating)** il gas; ~ **station** la stazione del servizio; ~ **(vehicle)** la benzina
gate (airport) l'uscita
gay gay; ~ **bar** il bar per gay; ~ **club** il club per gay
gel (hair) il gel
get off *v* **(a train/bus/subway)** scendere
get to *v* arrivare
gift il regalo; ~ **shop** il negozio di articoli da regalo
girl la ragazza; **~friend** la ragazza
give *v* dare
glass (drinking) il bicchiere; ~ **(material)** il vetro; **~es** gli occhiali
go *v* **(somewhere)** andare
gold l'oro
golf golf; ~ **course** il campo da golf; ~ **club** la mazza; ~ **tournament** la gara di golf
good *n* il bene; ~ *adj* buono; ~ **afternoon** buon pomeriggio; ~ **evening** buonasera; ~ **morning** buongiorno; ~ **bye** arrivederla; **~s** le merci
gram il grammo
grandchild il nipote
grandparent il nonno
gray grigio
green verde
grocery store il fruttivendolo
ground floor il pianterreno

groundcloth [ground-sheet BE] il telone impermeabile
group il gruppo
guide la guida; **~ book** la guida; **~ dog** il cane da guida
gym la palestra
gynecologist il ginecologo

H

hair i capelli; **~ dryer** l'asciugacapelli; **~ salon** il parrucchiere; **~brush** la spazzola ; **~ cut** il taglio; **~spray** la lacca; **~style** l'acconciatura, **~stylist** il parrucchiere
half la metà; **~ hour** la mezz'ora; **~-kilo** il mezzo chilo
hammer il martello
hand la mano; **~ luggage** il bagaglio a mano; **~bag** la borsetta
handicapped il disabile; **~ accessible** accessibile ai disabili
hangover la sbornia
happy felice
hat il cappello
have v avere
head (body part) la testa; **~ache** il mal di testa; **~phones** gli auricolari
health la salute; **~ food store**

l'erboristeria
heart il cuore; **~ condition** il disturbo cardiaco
heat il calore; **~er** il radiatore
hello salve
helmet il casco
help v aiutare; **~** n l'aiuto
here qui
heterosexual eterosessuale
hi ciao
high alto; **~chair** il seggiolone; **~-heeled shoes** le scarpe col tacco alto; **~way** l'autostrada
hiking boots gli scarponi da montagna
hill la collina
hire v [BE] noleggiare; **~ car [BE]** l'auto a noleggio
hitchhike v fare l'autostop
hockey l'hockey
holiday [BE] la vacanza
horse track l'ippodromo
hospital l'ospedale
hostel l'ostello
hot (temperature) caldo; **~ (spicy)** piccante; **~ springs** le terme; **~ water** l'acqua calda
hotel l'hotel
hour l'ora
house la casa; **~hold**

goods gli articoli casalinghi; **~keeping services** i servizi di pulizia domestica
how come; **~ much** quanto
hug v abbracciare
hungry affamato
hurt il dolore
husband il marito

I

ibuprofen l'ibuprofene
ice il ghiaccio; **~ hockey** l'hockey su ghiaccio
icy gelato
identification l'identificazione
ill malato
in in
include v includere
indoor pool la piscina interna
inexpensive a buon mercato
infected infetto
information (phone) le informazioni; **~ desk** l'ufficio informazioni
insect insetto; **~ bite** la puntura d'insetto; **~ repellent** il repellente per gli insetti
insert v inserire
insomnia l'insonnia
instant message il messaggio istantaneo
insulin l'insulina
insurance l'assicurazione;

~ card la tessera dell'assicurazione; **~ company** la compagnia di assicurazione
interesting interessante
intermediate intermedio
international (airport area) internazionale; **~ flight** il volo internazionale; **~ student card** la tessera internazionale dello studente
internet l'Internet; **~ cafe** l'Internet caffè; **~ service** il servizio Internet; **wireless ~** il collegamento wireless a Internet
interpreter l'interprete
intersection l'incrocio
intestine l'intestino
introduce v presentare
invoice [BE] la fattura
Ireland l'Irlanda
Irish irlandese
iron v stirare; **~** n **(clothes)** il ferro da stiro
Italian italiano
Italy l'Italia

J

jacket la giacca
jar il vaso
jaw la mascella
jazz il jazz; **~ club** il club jazz
jeans i jeans

jet ski l'acquascooter
jeweler il gioielliere
jewelry la gioielleria
join *v* unire
joint (body part) la
giuntura

K

key la chiave; **~ card**
la chiave elettronica;
~ ring il portachiavi
kiddie pool la piscina
per bambini
kidney (body part)
il rene
kilo il chilo; **~gram** il
chilogrammo; **~me-**
ter il chilometro
kiss *v* baciare
kitchen la cucina;
~ foil la carta
stagnola
knee il ginocchio
knife il coltello

L

lace il pizzo
lactose intolerant
intollerante al
lattosio
lake il lago
large grande
larger più grande
last ultimo
late (time) tardi
later più tardi
launderette [BE] la
lavanderia a gettone
laundromat la lavan-
deria a gettone
laundry la lavanderia;
~ facility il locale

lavanderia; **~ service**
il servizio di
lavanderia
lawyer l'avvocato
leather la pelle
leave *v* partire
left (direction) a
sinistra
leg la gamba
lens la lente
less meno
lesson la lezione
letter la lettera
library la biblioteca
life la vita; **~ jacket**
il giubbotto di
salvataggio; **~guard**
il bagnino
lift (ride) il passaggio;
~ [BE] l'ascensore;
~ pass il lift pass
light (overhead) la
lampada; **~** *v* **(ciga-**
rette) accendere;
~bulb la lampadina;
~er l'accendino
like *v* **(someone)**
piacere
line (train) la linea
linen il lino
lip il labbro
liquor store l'enoteca
liter il litro
little piccolo
live *v* vivere
liver (body part) il
fegato
loafers i mocassini
local locale
lock *v* chiudere; **~** *n*
la serratura
locker l'armadietto

log off *v* **(computer)**
fare il logoff
log on *v* **(computer)**
fare il logon
long lungo; **~ sleeves**
le maniche lunghe;
~-sighted [BE]
ipermetrope
look *v* guardare
lose *v* **(something)**
perdere
lost perso; **~ and**
found l'ufficio
oggetti smarriti
lotion la lozione
louder più forte
love *v* **(someone)**
amare; **~** *n* l'amore
low basso; **~er** più
basso
luggage il bagaglio;
~ cart il carrello
bagagli; **~ locker**
l'armadietto dei
bagagli; **~ ticket** lo
scontrino dei bagagli;
hand ~ [BE] il
bagaglio a mano
lunch il pranzo
lung il polmone

M

magazine la rivista
magnificent magnifico
mail *v* spedire; **~** *n* la
posta; **~box** la cas-
setta della posta
main principale; **~ at-**
traction l'attrattiva
principale; **~ course**
il piatto principale
make up [BE] (a

prescription)
il trucco
mall il centro com-
merciale
man l'uomo
manager il respon-
sabile
manicure il manicure
manual car l'auto col
cambio manuale
map la cartina
market il mercato
married sposato
marry *v* sposare
mass (church service)
la messa
massage il massaggio
match *n* **(wooden**
stick) il fiam-
mifero; **~** *n* **(game)**
la partita
meal il pasto
measure *v* **(someone/**
something) misura-
re; **~ing cup** la tazza
di misurazione; **~ing**
spoon il misurino
mechanic il mec-
canico
medicine la medicina
medium (size) medio
meet *v* **(someone)**
incontrare
meeting (corporate)
la riunione; **~ room**
sala riunioni
membership card la
tessera associativa
memorial (place) il
monumento
memory card la
scheda memoria

mend v riparare
menstrual cramp il crampo mestruale
menu il menù
message il messaggio
meter (parking) il parchimetro
microwave il microonde
midday [BE] mezzogiorno
midnight mezzanotte
mileage il chilometraggio
mini-bar il minibar
minute il minuto
missing (was never there) mancante; scomparso **(was previously there)**
mistake l'errore
mobile mobile; **~ home** la casa prefabbricata; **~ phone [BE]** il telefonino
mobility la mobilità
money il denaro
month il mese
mop lo spazzolone
moped lo scooter
more più
morning il mattino
mosque la moschea
mother la madre
motor il motore; **~ boat** il motoscafo; **~cycle** la motocicletta; **~way [BE]** l'autostrada
mountain la montagna; **~ bike** la mountain bike

mousse (hair) la mousse
mouth la bocca
movie il film; **~ theater** il cinema
mug v scippare
muscle il muscolo
museum il museo
music la musica; **~ store** il negozio di musica

N

nail l'unghia; **~ file** la lima; **~ salon** il salone di bellezza
name il nome
napkin il tovagliolo
nappy [BE] il pannolino
nationality la nazionalità
nature preserve la riserva naturale
(be) nauseous v avere la nausea
near vicino; **~-sighted** miope
neck il collo; **~lace** la collana
need v necessitare
newspaper il giornale
newsstand l'edicola
next prossimo
nice sympatico
night la notte; **~club** il nightclub
no no
non-alcoholic analcolico
non-smoking non fumatori

noon mezzogiorno
north nord
nose il naso
notes [BE] le banconote
nothing niente
notify v avvertire
novice il principiante
now ora
number il numero
nurse l'infermiere

O

office l'ufficio; **~ hours** l'orario d'ufficio
off-licence [BE] l'enoteca
oil l'olio
OK OK
old vecchio
on the corner all'angolo
once una volta
one uno; **~-way (ticket)** solo andata; **~-way street** il senso unico
only solo
open v aprire; **~** adj aperto
opera l'opera; **~ house** il teatro dell'opera
opposite di fronte a
optician l'ottico
orange (color) arancione
orchestra l'orchestra
order v ordinare
outdoor pool la piscina esterna
outside fuori

over sopra; **~ the counter (medication)** da banco; **~look (scenic place)** il belvedere; **~night** per la notte
oxygen treatment l'ossigeno terapia

P

p.m. del pomeriggio
pacifier il ciuccio
pack v fare le valigie
package il pacchetto
paddling pool [BE] la piscina per bambini
pad [BE] l'assorbente
pain il dolore
pajamas il pigiama
palace il palazzo
pants i pantaloni
pantyhose il collant
paper la carta; **~ towel** la carta da cucina
paracetamol [BE] il paracetamolo
park v parcheggiare; **~** n il parco; **~ing garage** il parcheggio; **~ing lot** il parcheggio
parliament building l'edificio del parlamento
part (for car) il ricambio; **~ time** part-time
pass through v passare
passenger il passeggero

passport il passaporto; **~ control** il controllo passaporti
password la password
pastry shop la pasticceria
path il sentiero
pay v pagare; **~ phone** il telefono pubblico
peak (of a mountain) la vetta
pearl la perla
pedestrian il pedone
pediatrician il pediatra
pedicure il pedicure
pen la penna
penicillin la penicillina
per per; **~ day** al giorno; **~ hour** all'ora; **~ night** a notte; **~ week** a settimana
perfume il profumo
period (menstrual) il ciclo; **~ (of time)** il periodo
permit v permettere
petite piccolo
petrol [BE] la benzina; **~ station [BE]** la stazione di servizio
pewter il peltro
pharmacy la farmacia
phone v telefonare; **~** n il telefono; **~ call** la telefonata; **~ card** la scheda telefonica; **~ number** il numero di telefono
photo la foto; **~copy**

la fotocopia; **~graphy** la fotografia
pick up v **(something)** raccogliere
picnic area la zona picnic
piece il pezzo
Pill (birth control) la pillola
pillow il cuscino
personal identification number (PIN) il codice PIN
pink rosa
piste [BE] la pista; **~ map [BE]** la cartina delle piste
pizzeria la pizzeria
place a bet v scommettere
plane l'aereo
plastic wrap la pellicola per alimenti
plate il piatto
platform (train) il binario
platinum il platino
play v giocare; **~** n **(theater)** lo spettacolo; **~ ground** il parco giochi; **~ pen** il box
please per favore
pleasure il piacere
plunger lo sturalavandini
plus size la taglia forte
pocket la tasca
poison il veleno
poles (skiing) le racchette

police la polizia; **~ report** il verbale di polizia; **~ station** il commissariato
pond lo stagno
pool (swimming) la piscina
pop music la musica pop
portion la porzione
post [BE] la posta; **~ office** l'ufficio postale; **~box [BE]** la buca delle lettere; **~card** la cartolina
pot (for cooking) la pentola; **~ (for flowers)** il vaso
pottery la ceramica
pounds (British sterling) le sterline
pregnant incinta
prescribe v prescrivere
prescription la ricetta
press v **(clothing)** stirare
price il prezzo
print v stampare
problem il problema
produce la frutta e verdura; **~ store** il fruttivendolo
prohibit v proibire
pronounce v pronunciare
public pubblico
pull v **(door sign)** tirare
purple viola
purse la borsetta
push v **(door sign)** spingere; **~chair**

[BE] il passeggino

Q

quality la qualità
question la domanda
quiet tranquillo

R

racetrack il circuito
racket (sports) la racchetta
railway station [BE] la stazione ferroviaria
rain la pioggia; **~coat** l'impermeabile; **~forest** la foresta pluviale; **~y** piovoso
rape v stuprare; **~** n lo stupro
rash l'irritazione
razor blade la lametta
reach v raggiungere
ready pronto
real vero
receipt la ricevuta
receive v ricevere
reception la reception
recharge v ricaricare
recommend v raccomandare
recommendation la raccomandazione
recycling il reciclaggio
red rosso
refrigerator il frigorifero
region la regione
registered mail la raccomandata
regular normale
relationship la relazione

rent *v* affittare
rental car l'auto a noleggio
repair *v* riparare
repeat *v* ripetere
reservation la prenotazione; **~ desk** l'ufficio prenotazioni
reserve *v* prenotare
restaurant il ristorante
restroom la toilette
retired in pensione
return *v* **(something)** portare indietro; **~** *n* **[BE]** la resa
rib (body part) la costola
right (direction) a destra; **~ of way** la precedenza
ring l'anello
river il fiume
road map la cartina stradale
rob *v* rubare; **~bed** derubato
romantic romantico
room la stanza; **~ key** la chiave della stanza; **~ service** il servizio in camera
round-trip l'andata e ritorno
route il percorso
rowboat la barca a remi
rubbish [BE] la spazzatura; **~ bag [BE]** il sacchetto per la spazzatura
rugby il rugby

ruins le rovine
rush la fretta

S

sad triste
safe (receptacle) la cassaforte; **~ (protected)** sicuro
sales tax l'IVA
same stesso
sandals i sandali
sanitary napkin l'assorbente
saucepan la pentola
sauna la sauna
save *v* **(computer)** salvare
savings (account) i risparmi
scanner lo scanner
scarf la sciarpa
schedule *v* programmare; **~** *n* il programma
school la scuola
science la scienza
scissors le forbici
sea il mare
seat il posto
security la sicurezza
see *v* vedere
self-service il self-service
sell *v* vendere
seminar il seminario
send *v* inviare
senior citizen l'anziano
separated (marriage) separato
serious serio
service (in a restau-

rant) il servizio
sexually transmitted disease (STD) la malattia sessualmente trasmissibile
shampoo lo shampoo
sharp appuntito
shaving cream la crema da barba
sheet (bedlinen) il lenzuolo; **~ (paper)** la pagina
ship *v* **(mail)** inviare
shirt la camicia
shoes le scarpe; **~ store** il negozio di calzature
shop *v* fare lo shopping
shopping lo shopping; **~ area** la zona commerciale; **~ centre [BE]** il centro commerciale; **~ mall** il centro commerciale
short corto; **~ sleeves** le maniche corte; **~s** i pantaloncini corti; **~-sighted [BE]** miope
shoulder la spalla
show *v* mostrare
shower la doccia
shrine il santuario
sick malato
side il lato; **~ dish** il contorno; **~ effect** l'effetto collaterale; **~ order** il contorno
sightseeing la visita turistica; **~ tour** la gita turistica

sign *v* firmare
silk la seta
silver l'argento
single (marriage) single; **~ bed** il letto a una piazza; **~ prints** le stampe singole; **~ room** la stanza singola
sink il lavandino
sister la sorella
sit *v* sedersi
size la taglia
skin la pelle
skirt la gonna
ski *v* sciare; **~** *n* lo sci; **~ lift** lo ski lift
sleep *v* dormire; **~er car** il vagone letto; **~ing bag** il sacco a pelo; **~ing car [BE]** il vagone letto
slice (of something) la fetta
slippers le ciabatte
slow lento; **~er** più lento; **~ly** lentamente
small piccolo; **~er** più piccolo
smoke *v* fumare
smoking (area) per fumatori
snack bar lo snack bar
sneakers le scarpe da ginnastica
snorkeling equipment l'attrezzatura da immersione
snow neve; **~board** lo snowboard; **~shoe** la scarpa da neve; **~y** nevoso

soap il sapone
soccer il calcio
sock il calzino
some qualche
soother [BE] il ciuccio
sore throat il mal
di gola
sorry scusi
south sud
souvenir il souvenir;
~ store il negozio di
souvenir
spa la stazione termale
spatula la spatola
speak v parlare
special (food) la spe-
cialità; **~ist (doctor)**
lo specialista
specimen il campione
speeding l'eccesso di
velocità
spell v scrivere
spicy piccante
spine (body part) la
spina dorsale
spoon il cucchiaio
sport lo sport; **~s
massage** il mas-
saggio sportivo
sporting goods store
il negozio di articoli
sportivi
sprain la storta
square quadrato;
**~ kilom-
eter** il chilometro
quadrato; **~ meter** il
metro quadrato
stadium lo stadio
stairs le scale
stamp v **(a
ticket)** convalidare;

~ n **(postage)** il
francobollo
start v iniziare
starter [BE] lo starter
station la stazione;
bus ~ la stazione dei
bus; **gas ~** il benzi-
naio; **petrol ~ [BE]**
il benzinaio; **railway
~ [BE]** la stazione
ferroviaria; **subway
~** la stazione della
metropolitana **train
~** la stazione ferrovi-
aria; **underground
~ [BE]** la stazione
della metropolitana;
~ wagon la station
wagon
statue la statua
stay v stare
steal v rubare
steep ripido
sterling silver
l'argento massiccio
sting la puntura
stolen rubato
stomach lo stomaco;
~ache il mal di
stomaco
stop v fermarsi; **~** n la
fermata
store directory la
piantina del negozio
storey [BE] il piano
stove la cucina
straight dritto
strange strano
stream il ruscello
stroller il passeggino
student lo studente
study v studiare

stunning fenomenale
subtitle il sottotitolo
subway la metro-
politana; **~ station**
la stazione della
metropolitana
suit l'abito; **~case** la
valigia
sun il sole; **~block**
il filtro solare;
~burn la scot-
tatura; **~glasses**
gli occhiali da sole;
~ny soleggiato;
~screen il
filtro solare; **~stroke**
l'insolazione
super (fuel) la super;
~market il super-
mercato; **~vision**
la supervisione
surfboard la tavola
da surf
swallow v ingoiare
sweater il maglione
sweatshirt la felpa
sweet (taste) dolce;
~s [BE] le cara-
melle
swelling il gonfiore
swim v nuotare; **~suit**
il costume da bagno
symbol (keyboard) il
simbolo
synagogue la
sinagoga

T

table il tavolo
tablet (medicine) la
compressa
take v prendere; **~**

away [BE] portare
via
tampon il tampone
taste v assaggiare
taxi il taxi
team la squadra
teaspoon il cucchiaino
telephone il telefono
temple (religious) il
tempio
temporary provvisorio
tennis il tennis
tent la tenda; **~ peg**
il picchetto da tenda;
~ pole il paletto
da tenda
terminal (airport) il
terminal
terracotta la ter-
racotta
terrible terribile
text v **(send a mes-
sage)** inviare SMS;
~ n **(message)** il
testo
thank v ringraziare; **~
you** grazie
that che
theater il teatro
theft il furto
there là
thief il ladro
thirsty assetato
this questo
throat la gola
ticket il biglietto; **~
office** la bigliette-
ria; **~ed passenger**
il passeggero con
biglietto
tie (clothing) la
cravatta

time il tempo; **~table [BE]** l'orario
tire lo pneumatico
tired stanco
tissue il fazzoletto di carta
tobacconist il tabaccaio
today oggi
toe il dito del piede; **~nail** l'unghia
toilet [BE] la toilette; **~ paper** la carta igienica
tomorrow domani
tongue la lingua
tonight stanotte
too troppo
tooth il dente; **~paste** il dentifricio
total (amount) il totale
tough (food) duro
tourist il turista; **~ information office** l'ufficio informazioni turistiche
tour la gita
tow truck il carro attrezzi
towel l'asciugamano
tower la torre
town la città; **~ hall** il municipio; **~ map** la cartina della città; **~ square** la piazza della città
toy il giocattolo; **~ store** il negozio di giocattoli
track (train) il binario
traditional tradizionale

traffic light il semaforo
trail il sentiero; **~ map** la mappa dei sentieri
trailer la roulotte
train il treno; **~ station** la stazione ferroviaria
transfer *v* **(change trains/flights)** cambiare; **~** *v* **(money)** trasferire
translate *v* tradurre
trash la spazzatura
travel viaggiare; **~ agency** l'agenzia viaggi; **~ sickness (air)** il mal d'aria; **~ sickness (car)** il mal d'auto; **~ sickness (sea)** il mal di mare; **~ers**
tree l'albero
trim (hair) una spuntatina
trip il viaggio
trolley [BE] il carrello
trousers i pantaloni
T-shirt la maglietta
turn off *v* spegnere
turn on *v* accendere
TV la TV
type *v* battere a macchina
tyre [BE] lo pneumatico

U

United Kingdom (U.K.) il Regno Unito
United States (U.S.)

gli Stati Uniti
ugly brutto
umbrella l'ombrello
unattended incustodito
unconscious inconscio
underground [BE] la metropolitana; **~ station [BE]** la stazione della metropolitana
underpants le mutande
understand *v* capire
underwear la biancheria intima
university l'università
unleaded (gas) senza piombo
upper superiore
upset stomach lo stomaco in disordine
urgent urgente
use *v* usare
username il nome utente

V

vacancy la disponibilità
vacation la vacanza
vaccination la vaccinazione
vacuum cleaner l'aspirapolvere
vaginal infection l'infezione vaginale
valid valido
valley la valle
valuable di valore
value il valore
VAT [BE] l'IVA

vegetarian vegetariano
vehicle registration il numero di targa
viewpoint la prospettiva
village il villaggio
vineyard il vigneto
visa il visto
visit *v* visitare; **~ing hours** gli orari di visita
visually impaired ipovedente
volleyball game la partita di pallavolo
vomit *v* vomitare

W

wait *v* attendere; **~** *n* l'attesa; **~ing room** la sala d'attesa
waiter il cameriere
waitress la cameriera
wake *v* svegliare, svegliarsi; **~-up call** il servizio sveglia
walk *v* camminare; **~** *n* la passeggiata; **~ing route** il percorso pedonale
wallet il portafogli
warm *v* **(something)** riscaldare; **~** *adj* **(temperature)** caldo
washing machine la lavatrice
watch l'orologio
water skis lo sci d'acqua
waterfall la cascata
weather il tempo

week la settimana;
~**end** il fine setti-
mana; ~**ly**
settimanalmente
welcome v accogliere
west ovest
what (question) cosa
wheelchair la sedia a
rotelle; ~ **ramp** la
rampa per sedia a
rotelle
when (question)
quando
where (question)
dove
white bianco; ~ **gold**
l'oro bianco
who (question) chi
widowed vedovo
wife la moglie
window la finestra; ~
case la vetrina
windsurfer il windsurf
wine list la carta
dei vini
wireless wireless; ~
internet l'Internet
wireless; ~ **internet**
service il servizio
Internet wireless; ~
phone il telefono
cordless
with con
withdraw v
ritirare; ~**al (bank)**
il prelievo
without senza
woman la donna
wool la lana
work v lavorare
wrap v incartare
wrist il polso
write v scrivere

Y

year l'anno
yellow giallo; ~ **gold**
l'oro giallo
yes sì
yesterday ieri
young giovane
youth hostel l'ostello
della gioventù

Z

zoo lo zoo

ITALIAN–ENGLISH

A

a buon mercato
inexpensive
a destra right
(direction)
a girocollo crew neck
a notte per night
a settimana per week
a sinistra left
(direction)
a tempo pieno
full-time
l'abbazia abbey
l'abbigliamento
clothing
abbracciare to hug
l'abito suit
accendere v light
(cigarette); ~ v turn
on (lights)
l'accendino lighter
accessibile ai disabili
handicapped- [disa-
bled BE] accessible
l'accesso access
accettare v accept
accogliere v welcome
l'acconciatura
hairstyle
l'acconto cash
advance
l'acqua water; ~ **calda**
hot water; ~ **potabile**
drinking water;
~**scooter** jet ski
l'adattatore adapter
addebitare v charge
(credit card)
l'aereo airplane
l'aeroporto airport
affamato hungry
affittare v rent
[hire BE]
l'agenzia agency; ~
viaggi travel agency
l'aggressione attack
(on person)
l'agopuntura acu-
puncture
l'AIDS AIDS
aiutare to help
l'aiuto n help
al giorno per day
l'albero tree
all'angolo on the
corner
allattare breastfeed
allergico allergic
l'alloggio accom-
modation
all'ora per hour
alto high
amare v love (someone)
l'ambulanza am-
bulance
americano American
l'amico friend
l'amore n love
analcolico non-
alcoholic
andare v go (some-
where); ~ **bene** fit
(clothing)
l'andata e ritorno
round-trip
l'anello ring
anemico anemic
l'anestesia anesthesia
l'animale animal
l'anno year
annullare v cancel
l'antibiotico antibiotic
l'antipasto appetizer
[starter BE]
l'anziano senior citizen
aperto adj open
l'appartamento apart-
ment
l'appendice appendix
(body part)
l'appuntamento
appointment

appuntito sharp

l'apribottiglie bottle opener

aprire v open

l'apriscatole can opener

arancione orange (color)

l'argento silver; ~ **massiccio** sterling silver

l'aria condizionata air conditioning

l'armadietto locker; ~ **dei bagagli** luggage locker

l'aromaterapia aromatherapy

arrivare v arrive

arrivederla goodbye

gli arrivi arrivals (airport)

l'arte art

l'arteria artery

gli articoli casalinghi household goods

l'artrite arthritis

l'ascensore elevator

l'asciugacapelli hair dryer

l'asciugamano towel

asmatico asthmatic

l'aspirapolvere vacuum cleaner

l'aspirina aspirin

assaggiare v taste

l'assegno n check (payment) [cheque BE]

assetato thirsty

l'assicurazione insurance

l'assorbente sanitary napkin [pad BE]

l'astuccio della macchina fotografica camera case

attendere v wait

l'attesa n wait

attraente attractive

l'attrattiva attraction (place); ~ **principale** main attraction

l'attrezzatura equipment; ~ **da immersione** snorkeling equipment; ~ **subacquea** diving equipment

gli auricolari headphones

Australia Australia

australiano Australian

l'auto car; **~bus** bus; ~ **con il cambio automatico** automatic car; ~ **con il cambio manuale** manual car; ~ **a noleggio** rental [hire BE] car

automatico automatic

l'autonoleggio car rental [hire BE]

l'autostrada highway [motorway BE]

avere v have; ~ **la nausea** v be nauseous

avvertire v notify

l'avvocato lawyer

B

la babysitter babysitter

baciare v kiss

il bagaglio luggage [baggage BE]; ~ **a mano** carry-on [hand luggage BE]

il bagnino lifeguard

il bagno bathroom

ballare v dance

il ballo dancing

il balsamo conditioner

il bambino child

la bambola doll

la banca bank

il bancomat ATM, ATM card, debit card

la banconota n bill (money) [note BE]

il bar bar; ~ **per gay** gay bar

il barbecue barbecue

il barbiere barber

la barca boat; ~ **a remi** rowboat

il baseball baseball

il basketball basketball

basso low

i bastoncini cinesi chopsticks

battere a macchina v type

la batteria battery

il bebè baby

beige beige

bello beautiful

il belvedere overlook (scenic place)

ben riposato well-rested

la benda bandage

bene good

la benzina gas (vehicle) [petrol BE]

il benzinaio gas [petrol BE] station

bere v drink

la bevanda n drink

la biancheria intima underwear

bianco white

il biberon baby bottle

la biblioteca library

il bicchiere glass (drinking)

la bicicletta bicycle

la biglietteria ticket office

il biglietto ticket; ~ **del bus** bus ticket; ~ **elettronico** e-ticket; ~ **da visita** business card

il bikini bikini

il binario platform; track (train)

blu blue

la bocca mouth

la borsa bag

la borsetta purse [handbag BE]

il bosco forest

la bottiglia bottle

il box playpen

il braccialetto bracelet

il braccio arm

bruciare v burn

brutto ugly

la buca delle lettere postbox

buongiorno good morning

buon pomeriggio good afternoon

buonasera good evening

buono _adj_ good
il bus espresso express bus
la busta envelope

C

il cabaret cabaret
la cabina cabin
il caffè cafe, coffee
il calcio soccer
caldo hot (temperature)
il calore heat (heating BE)
le calorie calories
il calzino sock
cambiare _v_ change; ~ _v_ exchange; ~ _v_ transfer
il cambio _n_ change (money); ~ _n_ exchange (place); ~ **valuta** currency exchange
la cameriera waitress
il cameriere waiter
la camicetta blouse
la camicia shirt
camminare _v_ walk
campeggiare _v_ camp
il campeggio campsite
il campione specimen
il campo field (sports); ~ **da golf** golf course; ~ **di battaglia** battleground
il Canada Canada
canadese Canadian
il canalone canyon
cancellare _v_ clear (on an ATM)

il cane da guida guide dog
i capelli hair
capire _v_ understand
il cappello hat
il cappotto coat
la caraffa carafe
le caramelle candy [sweet BE]
il carbone charcoal
carino cute
caro expensive
il carrello cart [trolley BE]; ~ **bagagli** luggage cart
il carro attrezzi tow truck
la carta card, paper; ~ **di credito** credit card; ~ **da cucina** paper towel; ~ **igienica** toilet paper; ~ **d'imbarco** boarding pass; ~ **stagnola** aluminum [kitchen BE] foil; ~ **dei vini** wine list
la cartina map; ~ **della città** town map; ~ **delle piste** trail [piste BE] map; ~ **stradale** road map
la cartolina postcard
il cartone carton
la casa house
la cascata waterfall
il casco helmet
il casinò casino
la cassa case (container); ~**forte** safe (for valuables)

la cassetta della posta mailbox
il cassiere cashier
il castello castle
la cattedrale cathedral
il cavatappi corkscrew
la caviglia ankle
il CD CD
Celsius Celsius
la cena dinner
il centimetro centimeter
il centro downtown area; ~ **business** business center; ~ **commerciale** shopping mall [centre BE]
la ceramica pottery
la ceretta wax; ~ **all'inguine** bikini wax; ~ **per sopracciglie** eyebrow wax
il certificato certificate
il cestino basket (grocery store)
che that
il check-in check-in (hotel/airport)
chi who
chiamare _v_ call
la chiamata _n_ call
la chiave key; ~ **elettronica** key card; ~ **della stanza** room key
la chiesa church
il chilo kilo; ~**grammo** kilogram; ~**metraggio** mileage;

~**metro** kilometer; ~**metro quadrato** square kilometer
chiudere _v_ close (a shop); ~ _v_ lock
chiuso closed
le ciabatte slippers
ciao hi, bye
il cibo food
il ciclismo cycling
il ciclo period (menstrual)
il cinema movie theater
cinese Chinese
la cintura belt
il circuito racetrack
la città town
il ciuccio pacifier [soother BE]
la classe class; ~ **business** business class; ~ **economica** economy class
il club club; ~ **di ballo** dance club; ~ **jazz** jazz club; ~ **per gay** gay club
il codice code; ~ **di abbigliamento** dress code; ~ **PIN** personal identification number (PIN)
la coincidenza connection (flight)
la colazione breakfast
la collana necklace
il collant pantyhose
il collega colleague
il collegamento connection (internet); ~ **wireless a Internet** wireless internet

collegarsi v connect (internet)
la collina hill
il collo neck
la colonia cologne
il colore color
il coltello knife
come how
il commissariato police station
la compagnia aerea airline
la compagnia di assi-curazione insurance company
compilare v fill out (form)
il compleanno birthday
comporre il numero v dial
comprare v buy
la compressa tablet (medicine)
il computer computer
con with
il concerto concert
la condizione condition (medical)
la conferenza conference
confermare v confirm
la congestione congestion
il consolato consulate
il consulente consultant
contagioso contagious
i contanti n cash
contattare to contact
il conto n bill (of sale); ~ account; ~

corrente checking [current BE] account
il contorno side dish
controllare v check (luggage)
il controllo passaporti passport control
convalidare v stamp (a ticket)
la coperta blanket
il coperto cover charge
la coppa bowl
il corridoio aisle
corto short
cosa what (question)
la coscia thigh
costare v cost
costipato constipated
il costo charge (cost)
la costola rib (body part)
il costume da bagno swimsuit
il cotone cotton
il crampo mestruale menstrual cramp
la cravatta tie (clothing)
la crema cream (oint-ment); ~ **antisettica** antiseptic cream; ~ **da barba** shaving cream
il cristallo crystal
la cuccetta berth
il cucchiaino teaspoon
il cucchiaio spoon
la cucina kitchen, stove
cucinare v cook
la culla crib

il cuore heart
il cuscino pillow

D

da banco over the counter (medication)
danneggiare v damage
danneggiato damaged
dare v give; ~ **da mangiare** v feed
la data date (calendar)
del pomeriggio p.m.
il denaro money
il dente tooth
la dentiera denture
il dentifricio toothpaste
il dentista dentist
il deodorante deodorant
depositare v deposit
il deposito n deposit
derubato robbed
il deserto desert
il detersivo detergent; ~ **per i piatti** dishwashing liquid
di fronte a opposite
di valore valuable
diabetico diabetic
il diamante diamond
la diarrea diarrhea
dichiarare v declare
il diesel diesel
dietro around (the corner), behind (direction)
difficile difficult
digitale digital
la direzione direction
il disabile handi-capped [disabled BE]

la disponibilità vacancy
il disturbo cardiaco heart condition
il dito finger; ~ **del piede** toe
divorziare v divorce
la doccia shower
la dogana customs
dolce sweet (taste)
il dollaro dollar (U.S.)
il dolore hurt (pain); ~ **al petto** chest pain
la domanda question
domani tomorrow
domestico domestic
la donna woman
dopo after; ~**barba** aftershave
doppiato dubbed
dormire v sleep
il dormitorio dormitory
dove where (question)
la dozzina dozen
dritto straight
durante during
duro tough (food)
duty-free duty-free
il DVD DVD

E

e and
l'eccesso excess; ~ **di velocità** speeding
economico cheap
l'edicola newsstand
l'edificio building; ~ **del parlamento** parliament building
l'effetto collaterale side effect

eliminare *v* delete (computer)
l'e-mail *n* e-mail
l'emergenza emergency
l'enoteca liquor store [off-licence BE]
entrare *v* enter
l'entrata entrance
l'erboristeria health food store
l'errore mistake
esausto exhausted
l'escursione excursion; **~ in pullman** bus tour
esperto expert
espresso express
essere *v* be
est east
estrarre *v* extract (tooth)
l'età age
l'euro euro
extra extra; **~ large** extra large

F

facile easy
la famiglia family
fare *v* do; **~ l'autostop** *v* hitchhike; **~ la ceretta** *v* wax; **~ un incidente** *v* crash (car); **~ il logoff** *v* log off (computer); **~ il logon** *v* log on (computer); **~ lo shopping** *v* shop; **~ le valigie** *v* pack
la farmacia pharmacy [chemist BE]
il fast food fast food
la fattoria farm
la fattura bill [invoice BE]
fatturare *v* bill (charge)
il fax *n* fax
il fazzoletto di carta tissue
la febbre fever
il fegato liver (body part)
felice happy
la felpa sweatshirt
fenomenale stunning
fermarsi *v* stop
la fermata *n* stop; **~ del bus** bus stop
il ferro da stiro *n* iron (clothes)
la fetta slice (of something)
il fiammifero *n* match (wooden stick)
il film movie
il filtro solare sunblock, sunscreen
il fine settimana weekend
la finestra window
finire *v* end
il fiore flower
firmare *v* sign
il fiume river
la fontana fountain
le forbici scissors
la forchetta fork
la foresta pluviale rainforest
il fornello da campeggio camping stove

la fortezza fort
la foto photo; **~ digitale** digital photo; **~copia** photocopy; **~grafia** photography
il francobollo *n* stamp (postage)
il fratello brother
freddo cold (temperature)
il freezer freezer
i freni brakes (car)
frequentare to attend
fresco cool (temperature); **~** fresh
la fretta rush
il frigorifero refrigerator
la frutta e verdura produce
il fruttivendolo grocery store
fumare *v* smoke
la funivia cable car
il fuoco fire
fuori outside
il furto theft; **~ con scasso** break-in (burglary)

G

la gamba leg
la gara di golf golf tournament
il garage garage
il gas gas (heating); **~ per cucina** cooking gas
la gastronomia delicatessen
gay gay
il gel gel (hair)

gelato icy
il ghiaccio ice
la giacca jacket
giallo yellow
il giardino botanico botanical garden
il ginecologo gynecologist
il ginocchio knee
giocare *v* play
il giocattolo toy
la gioielleria jewelry
il gioielliere jeweler
il giornale newspaper
il giorno day
giovane young
la gita tour; **~ turistica** sightseeing tour
il giubbotto di salvataggio life jacket
la giuntura joint (body part)
la goccia drop (medicine)
godersi *v* enjoy
la gola throat
il gomito elbow
la gomma rubber; **~ a terra** flat tire; **~ da masticare** chewing gum
il gonfiore swelling
la gonna skirt
i gradi degrees (temperature)
il grammo gram
grande big, large; **~ magazzino** department store
grazie thank you
grigio gray

la **grotta** cave
il **gruppo** group
guardare *v* look
il **guasto** breakdown
la **guida** guide, guide book
guidare *v* drive

H

l'**hockey** hockey; ~ **su ghiaccio** ice hockey
l'**hotel** hotel

I

l'**ibuprofene** ibuprofen
l'**identificazione** identification
ieri yesterday
imbarcarsi *v* board
l'**impermeabile** raincoat
in in; ~ **pensione** retired
incartare *v* wrap
incassare *v* cash
l'**incidente** accident
incidere *v* engrave
incinta pregnant
includere *v* include
inconscio unconscious
incontrare *v* meet (someone)
l'**incontro di boxe** boxing match
l'**incrocio** intersection
incustodito unattended
l'**indirizzo** address; ~ **e-mail** e-mail address
infastidire *v* bother

l'**infermiere** nurse
infetto infected
l'**infezione vaginale** vaginal infection
le **informazioni** information (phone)
inglese English
ingoiare *v* swallow
l'**ingresso** admission
iniziare *v* begin, start
inserire *v* insert
l'**insetto** bug
insipido bland
l'**insolazione** sunstroke
l'**insonnia** insomnia
l'**insulina** insulin
interessante interesting
intermedio intermediate
internazionale international (airport area)
l'**Internet** internet; ~ **caffè** internet cafe; ~ **wireless** wireless internet
l'**interno** extension (phone)
l'**interprete** interpreter
l'**intestino** intestine
intollerante al lattosio lactose intolerant
l'**intrattenimento** entertainment
inviare *v* send, ship (mail); ~ **e-mail** *v* e-mail; ~ **per fax** *v* fax; ~ **SMS** *v* text (send a message)

ipermetrope far- [long- BE] sighted
ipovedente visually impaired
l'**ippodromo** horsetrack
l'**Irlanda** Ireland
irlandese Irish
l'**irritazione** rash
l'**Italia** Italy
italiano Italian
l'**IVA** sales tax [VAT BE]

J

il **jazz** jazz
i **jeans** jeans

L

là there
la **casa prefabbricata** mobile home
la **stanza singola** single room
il **labbro** lip
la **lacca** hairspray
il **ladro** thief
il **lago** lake
la **lametta** razor blade; ~ **usa e getta** disposable razor
la **lampadina** lightbulb
la **lana** wool
il **latte in polvere** formula (baby)
il **lato** side
la **lavanderia** laundry; ~ **a gettone** laundromat [launderette BE]
il **lavandino** sink
il **lavasecco** dry

cleaner
la **lavastoviglie** dishwasher
la **lavatrice** washing machine
lavorare *v* work
il **lavoro** business
lentamente slowly
la **lente** lens; ~ **a contatto** contact lens
il **lenzuolo** sheet
la **lettera** letter
il **lettino** cot
il **letto** bed; ~ **matrimoniale** double bed; ~ **a una piazza** single bed
la **lezione** lesson
libero available, free
la **libreria** bookstore
il **libro** book
il **lift pass** lift pass
la **lima** nail file
la **linea** line (train)
la **lingua** tongue
il **lino** linen
il **litro** liter
locale local
lontano far
la **lozione** lotion
la **luce** light (overhead)
il **lunapark** amusement park
lungo long

M

la **macchina fotografica** camera; ~ **digitale** digital camera

il macellaio butcher
la madre mother
la maglietta T-shirt
il maglione sweater
magnifico magnificent
il mal sickness; **~ d'aria** motion sickness (air); **~ d'auto** motion sickness (car); **~ di gola** sore throat; **~ di mare** motion sickness (sea); **~ d'orecchio** earache; **~ di schiena** backache; **~ di stomaco** stomachache; **~ di testa** headache
malato sick [ill BE]
malattia sessualmente trasmissibile sexually transmitted disease (STD)
mancante missing
mangiare v eat
le maniche sleeves; **~ corte** short sleeves; **~ lunghe** long sleeves
il manicure manicure
la mano hand
il mare sea
il marito husband
marrone brown
il martello hammer
la mascella jaw
il massaggio massage; **~ sportivo** sports massage
il mattino morning

del mattino a.m.
il meccanico mechanic
la medicina medicine
il medico doctor
medio medium (size)
meno less
il menù menu; **~ delle bevande** drink menu; **~ per bambini** children's menu
il mercato market
le merci goods
il mese month
la messa mass (church service)
il messaggio message; **~ istantaneo** instant message
la metà half
il metro quadrato square meter
la metropolitana subway [underground BE]
la mezz'ora half hour
la mezzanotte midnight
il mezzo chilo half-kilo
mezzogiorno noon [midday BE]
il microonde microwave
migliore better
il migliore best
il minibar mini-bar
il minuto minute
miope near- [short- BE] sighted

misurare v measure (someone, something)
il misurino measuring spoon
mobile mobile
la mobilità mobility
i mocassini loafers
il mocio mop
modificare v alter (clothing)
il modulo form (fill-in)
la moglie wife
la moneta coin
la montagna mountain
il monumento memorial (place)
la moschea mosque
mostrare v show
la motocicletta motorcycle
il motore motor
il motoscafo motor boat
la mountain bike mountain bike
la mousse mousse (hair)
la multa fine (fee for breaking law)
il municipio town hall
il muscolo muscle
il museo museum
la musica music; **~ classica** classical music; **~ folk** folk music; **~ pop** pop music
le mutande underpants

N

il naso nose
il nastro trasportatore conveyor belt
le natiche buttocks
la nazionalità nationality
necessitare v need
il negozio store; **~ d'abbigliamento** clothing store; **~ d'antiquariato** antique store; **~ di articoli da regalo** gift shop; **~ di articoli sportivi** sporting goods store; **~ di calzature** shoe store; **~ di fotografia** camera store; **~ di giocattoli** toy store; **~ di musica** music store; **~ di souvenir** souvenir store
nero black
la neve snow
nevoso snowy
niente nothing
il nightclub nightclub
il nipote grandchild
no no
noioso boring
il nome name; **~ utente** username
non fumatori non-smoking
il nonno grandparent
nord north
normale regular
la notte night

il **numero** number; ~
  di fax fax number; ~
  di patente driver's
  license number; ~ **di**
  targa vehicle regis-
  tration; ~ **di telefono**
  phone number
nuotare v swim

O

gli **occhiali** glasses;
  ~ **da sole** sun-
  glasses
l'**occhio** eye
oggi today
OK OK
l'**olio** oil
l'**ombrello** umbrella
l'**opera** opera
ora now
l'**ora** hour
gli **orari di visita**
  visiting hours
l'**orario** schedule
  [timetable BE];
  ~ **d'apertura**
  business hours;
  ~ **d'ufficio** office
  hours
l'**orchestra** orchestra
ordinare v order
gli **orecchini** earrings
l'**orecchio** ear
l'**oro** gold; ~**bianco**
  white gold; ~ **giallo**
  yellow gold
l'**orologio** watch;
  ~ **da parete** wall
  clock
l'**ospedale** hospital
l'**osso** bone
l'**ostello** hostel; ~

  della gioventù
  youth hostel
l'**ottico** optician
l'**otturazione** filling
  (tooth)
ovest west

P

il **pacchetto** package
la **padella** frying pan
il **padre** father
il **pagamento del**
  conto check-out
  (hotel)
pagare v pay
il **palazzo** palace
la **palestra** gym
il **paletto da tenda**
  tent pole
la **panetteria** bakery
il **pannolino** diaper
  [nappy BE]
i **pantaloncini corti**
  shorts
i **pantaloni** pants
  [trousers BE]
il **paracetamolo**
  acetaminophen
  [paracetamol BE]
parcheggiare v park
il **parcheggio** parking
  garage; ~ parking
  lot [car park BE]
il **parco** n park; ~
  giochi playground
parlare v speak
il **parrucchiere** hair
  salon
le **partenze** departures
  (airport)
partire v leave
la **partita** game,

  match; ~ **di football**
  soccer [football game
  BE]; ~ **di pallavolo**
  volleyball game
part-time part-time
il **passaggio** lift
il **passaporto** passport
passare v pass
  through
il **passeggero** passen-
  ger; ~ **con biglietto**
  ticketed passenger
la **passeggiata** n walk
il **passeggino** stroller
  [pushchair BE]
la **password** password
la **pasticceria** pastry
  shop
il **pasto** meal
il **pediatra** pediatrician
il **pedicure** pedicure
il **pedone** pedestrian
la **pelle** leather, skin
la **pellicola per ali-**
  menti plastic wrap
  [cling film BE]
il **peltro** pewter
il **pene** penis
la **penicillina**
  penicillin
la **penna** pen
la **pensione** bed and
  breakfast
la **pentola** saucepan,
  pot
per for, per; ~ **favore**
  please; ~ **fumatori**
  smoking (area);
  ~ **la notte** overnight
il **percorso** route;
  ~ **alternativo**
  alternate route;

  ~ **ciclabile** bike
  route; ~ **pedonale**
  walking route
perdere v lose
  (something)
la **perdita** discharge
  (bodily fluid)
pericoloso dangerous
il **periodo** period (of
  time)
la **perla** pearl
permettere v allow,
  permit
perso lost
il **pettine** comb
il **petto** chest (body
  part)
il **petto** breast
il **pezzo** piece
piacere v like
il **piacere** pleasure
il **piano** floor [storey
  BE]
il **pianterreno** ground
  floor
la **piantina del**
  negozio store
  directory
il **piatto** plate; ~
  principale main
  course
la **piazza della città**
  town square
piccante hot (spicy)
il **picchetto da tenda**
  tent peg
piccolo little, petite,
  small
il **piede** foot
il **pigiama** pajamas
la **pillola** Pill (birth
  control)

la pioggia rain
piovoso rainy
la piscina pool; ~ **per bambini** kiddie [paddling BE] pool; ~ **esterna** outdoor pool; ~ **interna** indoor pool
pista piste [BE]
più more; ~ **basso** lower; ~ **economico** cheaper; ~ **forte** louder; ~ **grande** bigger; ~ **lento** slower; ~ **piccolo** smaller; ~ **tardi** later; ~ **veloce** faster
la pizzeria pizzeria
il pizzo lace
il platino platinum
lo pneumatico tire [tyre BE]
la polizia police
il polmone lung
il polso wrist
il pomeriggio afternoon
la pompa dell'aria air pump
il ponte bridge
la porta door; ~ **antincendio** fire door
il portachiavi key ring
il portafogli wallet
portare v bring; ~ **indietro** v return (something); ~ **via** to go [take away BE]
la porzione portion; ~ **per bambini** children's portion

la posa exposure (film)
la posta n mail [post BE]; ~ **aerea** airmail
il posto seat; ~ **sul corridoio** aisle seat
il pranzo lunch
la precedenza right of way
il prefisso area code; ~ **del paese** country code
il prelievo withdrawal (bank)
prendere v take
prenotare v reserve
la prenotazione reservation
la presa elettrica electric outlet
prescrivere v prescribe
presentare v introduce
il preservativo condom
la pressione sanguigna blood pressure
presto early
la previsione forecast
il prezzo price
prima before, earlier; ~ **classe** first class
primo first
il principiante beginner, novice
il problema problem
i prodotti per la pulizia cleaning supplies
profondamente deeply
il profumo perfume
il programma n

schedule
programmare v schedule
proibire v prohibit
pronto ready
pronunciare v pronounce
la prospettiva viewpoint
prossimo next
provvisorio temporary
pubblico public
pulire v clean
pulito adj clean
la pulizia del viso facial
la puntura sting; ~ **d'insetto** insect bite

Q

quadrato square
qualche some
la qualità quality
qualsiasi cosa anything
quando when (question)
quanto how much (question)
questo this
qui here

R

la racchetta racket (sports)
le racchette poles (skiing)
raccogliere v pick up (something)
raccomandare v recommend
la raccomandata

registered mail
la raccomandazione recommendation
il radiatore heater
il raffreddore cold (sickness)
la ragazza girl, girlfriend
il ragazzo boy, boyfriend
raggiungere v reach (get hold of)
il rame copper
la rampa per sedia a rotelle wheelchair ramp
il rap rap (music)
la reazione allergica allergic reaction
la reception reception
il reclamo complaint
il regalo gift
il reggiseno bra
la regione region
il Regno Unito United Kingdom (U.K.)
la relazione relationship
il rene kidney (body part)
il repellente per gli insetti insect repellent
il residente UE EU resident
respirare v breathe
il ricambio part (for car)
il riciclaggio n recycling
la ricetta prescription
ricevere v receive

la ricevuta receipt
il riciclaggio *n* recycling
riempire *v* fill
rifiutare *v* decline (credit card)
ringraziare *v* thank
riparare *v* fix, mend, repair
ripetere *v* repeat
ripido steep
il responsabile manager
il riscaldamento heating
riscaldare *v* warm (something)
la riserva naturale nature preserve
i risparmi savings (account)
il ristorante restaurant
ritardare *v* delay
ritirare *v* withdraw
il ritiro bagagli baggage claim
la riunione meeting
la rivista magazine
romantico romantic
rompere *v* break
rosa pink
rosso red
rotto broken
la roulotte trailer
le rovine ruins
rubare *v* rob, steal
rubato stolen
il rugby rugby
il rullino film (camera)
il ruscello stream

S

il sacchetto per i rifiuti garbage [rubbish BE] bag
il sacco a pelo sleeping bag
la sala room; **~ congressi** convention hall; **~ d'attesa** waiting room; **~ da concerti** concert hall; **~ da pranzo** dining room; **~ giochi** arcade; **~ riunioni** meeting room
il salone di bellezza nail salon
la salute health
Salute! Cheers!
salvare *v* save (computer)
salve hello
la salvietta per neonati baby wipe
i sandali sandals
il sangue blood
sanguinare *v* bleed
il santuario shrine
il sapone soap
la sauna sauna
la sbornia hangover
le scale stairs; **~ mobili** escalators
lo scanner scanner
le scarpe shoes; **~ da neve** snowshoes; **~ basse** flat shoes; **~ col tacco alto** high-heeled shoes; **~ da ginnastica** sneakers
gli scarponi da montagna hiking boots
la scatola box
lo scatolame canned good
scendere *v* get off (a train, bus, subway)
la scheda card; **~ memoria** memory card; **~ telefonica** phone card
lo schermo display
la schiena back (body part)
lo sci *n* ski; **~ d'acqua** water skis
sciare *v* ski
la sciarpa scarf
la scienza science
scippare *v* mug
la scogliera cliff
la scolapasta colander
scollegare *v* disconnect (computer)
lo scollo a V V-neck
scommettere *v* place a bet
scomparso missing
lo sconto discount
lo scontrino bagagli luggage [baggage BE] ticket
lo scooter moped
la scopa broom
la scottatura sunburn
scrivere *v* spell, write
la scuola school
scuro dark
scusare *v* excuse
scusi sorry (apology)
sedersi *v* sit

la sedia chair; **~ a rotelle** wheelchair; **~ a sdraio** deck chair
il sedile per bambino child's seat
il seggiolino per auto car seat
il seggiolone highchair
la seggiovia chair lift
il self-service self-service
il semaforo traffic light
il seminario seminar
il senso unico one-way street
il sentiero path, trail
senza without; **~ grassi** fat free; **~ piombo** unleaded (gas)
separato separated (marriage)
la sera evening
serio serious
la serratura *n* lock
i servizi di pulizia domestica housekeeping services
il servizio service (in a restaurant); **~ completo** full-service; **~ di lavanderia** laundry service; **~ in camera** room service; **~ Internet** internet service; **~ Internet wireless** wireless internet service; **~ sveglia** wake-up call

la seta silk
la settimana week
settimanalmente
    weekly
lo shampoo shampoo
lo shopping shopping
sì yes
la sicurezza security
sicuro safe (protected)
la sigaretta cigarette
il sigaro cigar
il simbolo symbol
    (keyboard)
la sinagoga syna-
    gogue
single single (marriage)
lo ski lift drag lift,
    ski lift
lo slip briefs (clothing)
lo smalto enamel
    (jewelry)
lo snack bar snack bar
lo snowboard
    snowboard
il sole sun
soleggiato sunny
solo alone, only; **~
    andata** one-way
    (ticket)
**la soluzione per lenti
    a contatto** contact
    lens solution
la sonnolenza
    drowsiness
sopra over
sordo deaf
la sorella sister
il sottotitolo subtitle
il souvenir souvenir
la spalla shoulder
la spatola spatula
la spazzatura trash

[rubbish BE]
la spazzola hairbrush
lo specialista special-
    ist (doctor)
la specialità special
    (food)
spedire v mail
spegnere v turn off
    (lights)
lo spettacolo n play
    (theater); **~ di danza**
    ballet
la spiaggia beach
la spilla brooch
la spina dorsale
    spine (body part)
spingere v push (door
    sign)
lo spogliatoio fitting
    room
sporco dirty
lo sport sport
sposare v marry
sposato married
la spuntatina trim
    (hair)
la squadra team
squisito delicious
lo stadio stadium
lo stagno pond
stampare v print
la stampa n print;
    ~ digitale digital
    print; **~ singola**
    single print
stanco tired
stanotte tonight
la stanza room
stare v stay
gli Stati Uniti United
    States (U.S.)
la station wagon

station wagon [estate
    car BE]
la statua statue
la stazione station; **~
    degli autobus** bus
    station; **~ dei bus**
    bus station; **~ fer-
    roviaria** train station
    [railway station BE]; **~
    della metropolitana**
    subway station [un-
    derground station BE];
    ~ di servizio gas
    station [petrol station
    BE]; **~ termale** spa
la stecca di sigarette
    carton of cigarettes
le sterline pounds
    (British sterling)
stesso same
stirare v iron, press
    (clothing)
gli stivali boots
lo stomaco stomach;
    ~ in disordine
    upset stomach
stordito dizzy
la storta sprain
strano strange
straordinario amazing
lo studente student
studiare v study
stuprare v rape
lo stupro n rape
lo sturalavandini
    plunger
sud south
la super super (fuel)
superiore upper
il supermercato
    supermarket
la supervisione

supervision
svegliare, svegliarsi
    v wake
sviluppare v develop
    (film)
svuotare v empty

T

il tabaccaio tobac-
    conist
la taglia size; **~ forte**
    plus size
tagliare v cut (hair)
il taglio n cut (injury),
    haircut
il tampone tampon
tardi late (time)
la tariffa fee
la tasca pocket
la tassa duty (tax)
il tasso di cambio
    exchange rate
la tavola da surf
    surfboard
il tavolo table
il taxi taxi
la tazza cup; **~
    di misurazione**
    measuring cup
il teatro theater; **~
    dell'opera** opera
    house
telefonare v phone
la telefonata phone
    call
il telefonino cell
    [mobile BE] phone
il telefono n phone;
    **~ telephone; ~
    cordless** wireless
    phone; **~ pubblico**
    pay phone

**il telone impermea-
bile** groundcloth
[groundsheet BE]
il tempio temple
(religious)
il tempo time, weather
la tenda tent
il tennis tennis
la terapia ad ossigeno
oxygen treatment
le terme hot spring
il terminal terminal
(airport)
la terracotta ter-
racotta
terribile terrible
la tessera card;
~ associativa
membership card;
**~ dell'assicura-
zione** insurance
card; **~ internazion-
ale dello studente**
international student
card
la testa head (body
part)
il testo n text (mes-
sage)
tirare v pull (door sign)
la toilette restroom
[toilet BE]
la torcia elettrica
flashlight
la torre tower
la tosse n cough
tossire v cough
il totale total (amount)
il tovagliolo napkin
tradizionale tradi-
tional
tradurre v translate

il traghetto ferry
tranquillo quiet
trasferire v transfer
(money)
il travellers cheque
travelers check
[travelers cheque BE]
il treno train; **~
espresso** express
train
triste sad
troppo too
tuffarsi v dive
il turista tourist
la TV TV

U

l'uccello bird
l'ufficio office; **~ di
cambio** currency
exchange office;
~ informazioni
information desk;
**~ informazioni
turistiche** tourist
information office;
~ oggetti smarriti
lost and found; **~
postale** post of-
fice; **~ prenotazioni**
reservation desk
ultimo last
una volta once
l'unghia fingernail,
toenail
unire v join
l'università university
uno one
l'uomo man
urgente urgent
usa e getta disposable
usare v use

uscire v exit
l'uscita gate (airport),
exit; **~ d'emergenza**
emergency exit
l'utensile utensil

V

la vacanza vacation
[holiday BE]
la vaccinazione vac-
cination
la vagina vagina
il vagone letto
sleeper [sleeping
BE] car
valido valid
la valigia suitcase
la valle valley
il valore value
la valuta currency
il vaso jar
vecchio old
vedere v see
vedovo widowed
vegetariano veg-
etarian
il veleno poison
veloce fast
vendere v sell
venire v come
il ventaglio fan
(souvenir)
il ventilatore fan
(appliance)
il verbale di polizia
police report
verde green
vero real
la vescica bladder
il vestito dress (piece
of clothing)
la vetrina window

case
la vetrinetta display
case
il vetro glass
(material)
la vetta peak (of a
mountain)
il viaggio trip
vicino close, near,
nearby, next to
i vigili del fuoco fire
department
il vigneto vineyard
il villaggio village
viola purple
la visita turistica
sightseeing
visitare v visit
il viso face
il visto visa
la vita life
la vitamina vitamin
vivere v live
il volo flight; **~
internazionale**
international flight; **~
nazionale** domestic
flight
vomitare v vomit

W

il WC da campeggio
chemical toilet
il windsurf windsurfer

Z

lo zaino backpack
la zona area; **~ com-
merciale** shopping
area; **~ picnic** picnic
area
lo zoo zoo

INDEX

Berlitz® pocket guide

SARDINIA

Fifth Edition 2020

Editor: Carine Tracanelli
Author: Susie Boulton
Head of DTP and Pre-Press: Rebeka Davies
Managing Editor: Carine Tracanelli
Picture Editor: Tom Smyth
Layout: Aga Bylica
Cartography Update: Carte
Update Production: Apa Digital
Photography Credits: Getty Images 1, 4ML, 5M, 26, 98; iStock 4MC, 4TL, 5TC, 11, 12, 15, 16, 20, 40, 44, 52, 59, 68, 70, 82, 84, 88, 93, 96, 101, 104; Shutterstock 5MC, 6R, 7R, 39, 43, 73, 74, 79, 106; Sylvaine Poitau/Apa Publications 4TC, 5T, 5M, 5MC, 6L, 7, 14, 19, 23, 24, 29, 31, 33, 35, 36, 46, 48, 50, 54, 56, 60, 63, 64, 66, 77, 81, 87, 91, 94, 95, 103
Cover Picture: iStock

Distribution
UK, Ireland and Europe: Apa Publications (UK) Ltd; sales@insightguides.com
United States and Canada: Ingram Publisher Services; ips@ingramcontent.com
Australia and New Zealand: Woodslane; info@woodslane.com.au
Southeast Asia: Apa Publications (SN) Pte; singaporeoffice@insightguides.com
Worldwide: Apa Publications (UK) Ltd; sales@insightguides.com

Special Sales, Content Licensing and CoPublishing
Insight Guides can be purchased in bulk quantities at discounted prices. We can create special editions, personalised jackets and corporate imprints tailored to your needs. sales@insightguides.com; www.insightguides.biz

Contact us
Every effort has been made to provide accurate information in this publication, but changes are inevitable. The publisher cannot be responsible for any resulting loss, inconvenience or injury. We would appreciate it if readers would call our attention to any errors or outdated information. We also welcome your suggestions; please contact us at: berlitz@apaguide.co.uk www.insightguides.com/berlitz